What the experts are saying about
One Minute Mysteries:
65 <u>More</u> Short Mysteries You Solve With Science!

One Minute Mysteries:
65 <u>More</u> Short Mysteries You Solve With Science!

Eric Yoder and Natalie Yoder

Science, Naturally!®
Washington, DC

Published in the United States by:
        Science, Naturally!® LLC
        725 8th Street, SE
        Washington, DC 20003
        202-465-4798 / Toll-free: 1-866-SCI-9876 (1-866-724-9876)
        Fax: 202-558-2132
        Info@ScienceNaturally.com / www.ScienceNaturally.com

Distributed to the book trade in the United States by:
        National Book Network
        301-459-3366 / Toll-free: 800-787-6859 / Fax: 301-429-5746
        CustServ@nbnbooks.com / www.nbnbooks.com

Senior Editor: Erin Friedlander

Editors: Michael Oshinsky
                Will Fenstermaker
                Zoe Waltz
                Ashley Parker
                Nicole Atallah
                Jacqueline Drayer

Cover, Book Design and Section Illustrations by Andrew Barthelmes, Peekskill, NY

Library of Congress Cataloging-in-Publication Data

Yoder, Eric.
  65 more mysteries you solve with science! / Eric and Natalie Yoder. -- First edition.
     pages cm -- (One minute mysteries)
  Audience: Age 8-12.
  Includes index.
  ISBN 978-1-938492-00-6 -- ISBN 1-938492-00-5 -- ISBN 978-1-938492-01-3 (ebook) (print) -- ISBN
1-938492-01-3 (ebook) (print) 1. Science--Methodology--Juvenile literature. 2. Science--Miscellanea--
Juvenile literature. 3. Science--Study and teaching (Middle school)--Juvenile literature. 4. Detective and
mystery stories. I. Yoder, Natalie, 1993- II. Title. III. Title: Sixty-five more mysteries you solve with science!
  Q173.Y633 2012
  507.1'2--dc23
                            2012032155

10 9 8 7 6 5 4 3 2 1

Schools, libraries, government and non-profit organizations can receive a bulk discount for quantity
orders. Please contact us at the address above or email us at Info@ScienceNaturally.com.

Printed in the United States of America

All characters in this book are the product of the authors' imaginations and are not real people. Any resemblance to those living now or in the past is a coincidence.

Supporting and Articulating Curriculum Standards

The content in all *Science, Naturally!* books correlates directly with the math and science standards laid out by the Center for Education at the National Academies. The articulation of the standards met by each mystery is available at www.ScienceNaturally.com.

Table of Contents

Physical and Chemical Science ●————(79)

General Science ●————————(111)

Why I Wrote This Book–
by Eric Yoder

When Natalie and I set out to write this book, the third in our "One Minute Mysteries" series, it was a different process. Our first two books had strong sales and we had to make sure that this next book did not repeat the themes in either the first science or math book. Also, Natalie was a middle school student and budding writer for the first book, a high school student for the second, and now she is in college, much more adept at writing. Continuing to write together has helped shape and grow our relationship.

As with the first book, I wanted to emphasize the widespread, real-life applications of science. Fortunately, the topic of science is virtually endless, especially from a young reader's perspective, so we had a lot of material to work with. So much of what happens in the world around us reveals its underlying science...if we just take the time to think about it. And once you think, you're more likely to explore. All of us could stand to do more of both!

Creating these books brings us a lot of pleasure. We hope you'll enjoy the journey through these stories and that they will inspire you to make discovery a part of your daily life.

–Eric

Why I Wrote This Book–
by Natalie Yoder

Writing these books was a great experience as a middle school and high school student. It definitely expanded my writing skills and helped prepare me for college. Through this writing process, I learned how to put a story with a twist into a small number of words and to create characters and settings.

Writing each book has been a different experience. I especially enjoyed writing this book because, after years of creating mysteries, we'd already stashed away a bunch of story ideas, and when we got stuck we still had fun bouncing ideas off of each other. We've become more efficient at writing and editing the stories. We've become good at understanding how a story has to flow and we can easily pick out which ideas aren't going to make it. I grew up learning that practice makes perfect, and now I know that is especially true of writing!

Creating these books has been a highlight of my life. It makes me happy that kids love them. Writing is a great skill and it lets you communicate with the world. At any age, you can write if you set your mind to it. It doesn't matter what you write about, just write.

– Natalie

Life Science

Cool as a Cucumber

When Alex and Iona planted a vegetable garden the previous year, their dog, Trevor, discovered how much he liked to jump over the barrier and destroy the plants. Cucumbers were Trevor's favorite. He would get at the cucumbers just as they were starting to ripen. Pulling the young cucumbers off their vines, he would stretch out in the sunshine of the yard and eat them.

Now it was time to plant this year's garden, so Alex and Iona went with their father to the hardware store to pick up seeds and fertilizer.

"I have an idea," Alex said, disappearing down a hardware aisle. He came back with some wooden stakes and a roll of the fine wire mesh used for window screens.

"What do you plan to do with those things?" their father asked.

"I'm going to build a cage to protect the cucumber plants," Alex said. "I'll make it strong and have the plants totally covered, all the way around from the ground and across the top. Then there will be no way Trevor can get at the cucumbers."

"I'm afraid if you do that, we still won't have cucumbers on our salads this year," Iona said.

"The plants will still get water and sunshine. That's all they need to grow, isn't it?" Alex wondered.

"That's all the plants need, sure. But to grow cucumbers, they also need something else."

"What could that be?"

"The plants would start to grow," Iona said. "But for the plants to produce cucumbers, they first put out flowers. Those flowers need to be pollinated, and insects do that. If there is no way for the insects to get to the flowers to pollinate them, the cucumbers won't grow. Let's get a kind of wire mesh that has holes big enough to let insects in, but that will still keep Trevor out."

Whale of a Time

"I'm so happy that we decided to take this whale-watching tour!" Matt managed to yell to his parents over the sound of the engine as the boat moved rapidly through the waters of the Atlantic Ocean.

They had agreed to take him on the tour after he had been studying biology the whole year. He had a passion for learning about marine animals and wanted to see them in the wild. His little sister Abigail had come along, too.

The boat slowed down and the engine finally stopped. The captain came out on the deck and joined them.

"We're in their migration route. Keep watching," he said, and went back to the controls.

After a long time had passed, Matt started worrying that they would never see any whales. The captain had said there was no guarantee. However, he suddenly called the passengers to join him in the control room.

"Look at this," he said, pointing to a screen with large dots on it. "This is sonar, which uses sound to detect anything in the water. There are whales headed our way."

Abigail said, "But fish can just stay under the water. Maybe they'll never come up and we won't see them."

"Let's go out on the deck to watch. They'll come up," Matt said.

"What makes you so sure?" she asked.

"Whales aren't fish," Matt said. "They're mammals, and they breathe air. They can hold their breath for a long time, but eventually they have to come to the surface for fresh air. When they take a breath they first blow out the old air, sending some water up with it. That's what we can look for. Fish, on the other hand, get their oxygen from the water through gills, so they don't need to come up for air."

Back to Nature

Hayden and Audrey's family had moved during the summer when their mother started working in a rural health clinic. Now, several months into the school year, they had gotten to know many of the families on the farms around them. Most of them did not live within walking distance so they had to ride their bikes to visit them.

Their four friends who lived within biking distance all had farms on which they grew trees. Wyatt's family had apple and peach trees. Henry's family grew oak trees for landscaping and Malcolm's family specialized in decorative maple trees. Carson's family, who lived the farthest away, had acres of Christmas trees around his house.

Audrey was watering flowers in the front yard when Hayden pulled up the driveway on his bike.

"I thought you'd be back a while ago," she said. "What were you doing?"

"Mainly watching animals at a friend's place. Birds, rabbits, a bunch of squirrels gathering acorns..." he said. "Living here is really different than living in the city. I'm really starting to get into all this nature stuff."

"I am, too! In fact, I bet I know whose house you were at simply based on what you said," she said.

"No way. I bet you don't!" he retorted.

"You're on! Loser does the dishes tonight."

"Okay, but you only get one guess. Where was I?" he asked.

"You were at Henry's house," Audrey said. "Maple trees, Christmas trees and fruit trees don't produce acorns, but oak trees do. Squirrels are very active at this time of year, gathering and storing them for the winter. Am I right, or am I right?"

"Fine, you're right. I guess I'll do the dishes tonight," Hayden conceded.

④ The Root of the Situation

"Daisuke, don't forget to water my plant while I'm gone!" his sister Miyu reminded him as she left the house.

Daisuke had agreed to take care of Miyu's plant during the weeks that she would be away on a concert tour with her high school chorus. She kept the plant inside their screened-in porch, where it got sunlight, but not rain. She had told her little brother it needed to be watered regularly in the hot summer weather.

Daisuke got a spray bottle and sprayed the leaves every day. After a few days, he wanted to prove to his sister that he had been taking care of her plant, so he asked his mother to send her a picture of the plant with the sprayer he used next to it.

That night when Miyu called she asked to talk to Daisuke.

"That plant looks droopy," Miyu said. "Are you sure you're taking care of it?"

"I water it every day," Daisuke said defensively.

"Dad, could you help Daisuke with the plant?" Miyu asked when their father took the phone from Daisuke.

"I haven't been watching him," their father said. "What do you think he is doing wrong?"

"I don't think he's giving it enough water," Miyu said.

Their father went out on the porch with Daisuke and checked the soil. It was almost completely dry.

"You're right," their father said before he handed the phone back to Daisuke and went to the kitchen to get more water for the plant.

"What did I do wrong?" Daisuke asked Miyu on the phone.

"Daisuke," Miyu said, "plants need water, nutrients and sunlight to grow. They get sunlight through their leaves, but most of the water and nutrients they need come through their roots. Some plants can absorb enough water to survive through their leaves, but most plants need to be watered at the roots. So when I saw the spray bottle but no other water container, I knew what was wrong. If you were misting it every day and it still needed water, you must have been only spraying the leaves, and not putting water at the roots where it could be more easily absorbed."

Shoo Fly, Don't Bother Me

"Are you sure you have everything?" Luke's mother called from the kitchen. He was waiting by the front door to join some friends for the walk to school.

"Yes, Mom. Sunscreen, bug spray, clothes, toothbrush and all that," he said.

"How about a snack for the bus ride?"

"I am bringing an apple and I even sealed it in a plastic bag to protect it."

Luke and his class were headed to an overnight nature camp where their biology class had a chance to explore the concepts that they had been learning about in the classroom.

He wasn't hungry on the bus ride, so he just left his apple in its bag in his backpack.

They spent the rest of the day and the next morning learning about nature. When it was time for lunch, Luke got a sandwich and took out the apple he had brought with him. He sat down with some friends to eat, but when he opened the bag, small flies flew out.

"Gross!" Luke said. "There are bugs on my apple! That's so weird."

"What's so weird about bugs?" his friend Elias asked.

"They weren't in the bag when I sealed it, and they couldn't have gotten in afterward. They must have appeared out of thin air! Where else could they have come from?" Luke asked.

"The bugs didn't come from thin air," Elias explained. "There used to be this idea called 'spontaneous generation' where people thought that living things like flies could grow straight out of non-living things like rotting food, but science has proven it wrong. Fruit flies must have laid eggs on that apple sometime before you put it in the bag. Since then, the eggs must have hatched into larvae and the larvae must have completed their metamorphosis. Fruit flies have a very fast life cycle."

"I guess my mom is right," Luke said. "You really do need to wash fruit before you eat it!"

Think Outside the Box

It was lunchtime at school, and Axel was sitting in the cafeteria with a few of his friends, staring at the last few pieces of pizza in the delivery box. It was a pizza with green peppers that his friend Peter's mom had brought in for his birthday, the only time the school allowed lunch food to be brought in for students.

As Peter reached for another piece, he casually asked, "So, how did everyone's cell model project go? It's due next period, right?"

"Oh no!" Axel said, his heart dropping as a sudden feeling of anxiety rose within him. "That's due next period? I completely forgot! What is the assignment again?"

Peter reached into his backpack and took out the assignment sheet. "Construct and label a model representing either a plant or animal cell, describing the functions of at least four parts of the cell," he read. "But how are you going to manage to make a cell model before next period? Lunch ends in ten minutes!" Peter exclaimed as he picked up another piece of pizza and dipped it in some garlic butter.

"Wait, don't be so negative," Axel said. "We have to make the best of every situation, right? I know what kind of cell I'm going to make. And I have enough materials right here to represent four cell parts."

"With what?" Peter asked. "All we have is the pizza scraps and an empty box."

Axel said, "Well, we have this pizza box, which has hard sides. That means I have to make this a plant cell. Plant cells have hard cell walls, but animal cells don't—they only have cell membranes. The cell wall allows water and nutrients into the cell. That's one part.

"I can use the green peppers we have left to represent chloroplasts, which help a plant cell convert sunlight into energy," he continued. "Chloroplasts are green because they contain chlorophyll. Also, they're found only in plant cells, not animal cells. And we have liquid garlic butter, which I can spill in the bottom of the box to represent the cytoplasm, which is a liquid that contains other cell structures. Once we empty out the garlic butter container, it can become the vacuole, which stores nutrients and minerals. That's four accurate parts of a plant cell. Then all I have to do is label them and write the descriptions."

"But first we have to finish eating this pizza," he added, pausing dramatically, "just not the green peppers!"

Now You See It

In the final challenge for the Cabin of the Week prize, the campers had to put all of their brain power together.

Isabel and her cabin mates went to the arts and crafts tent, where rolls of cloth were awaiting them—gray, green, and tan.

"Your challenge is to put on a short play tonight about life in the forest here at camp. You must stick to that theme in your costume and behavior," the counselor said. "Use this cloth for anything you want to make."

"We need something classy, but not overdone," Isabel said when the counselor left them with the supplies. "Something that fits the theme and that we can put together fast."

"We need to be able to show the lives of the animals," Grace said. "Maybe show what they eat? No, that's too complicated."

Some other girls had ideas, but nothing seemed good enough to win the challenge.

Then Melissa said, "Maybe we could do a play that shows how animals keep themselves safe?"

"Well, a lot of animals rely on speed to outrun a predator, others have claws and teeth to fight back, others have really good senses to detect danger," Anita said. "But how can we show one of those ideas with just colored cloth?"

"I was thinking about another way animals are protected: camouflage," Melissa said. "We can put on a play about how some animals blend in with their surroundings to make it harder to find them. We already have the colors of nature, and it's easy to also use the colors we have to show how animals blend in with their environment."

"I like it," Isabel said. "The gray cloth can be used to make tree trunks and squirrel outfits, the green could be used to make a lily pad and a frog. The tan can be used for grasses and deer."

8 Here Today, Gone Tomorrow

"Let's go straight to that field with the elk," Dominic said as he and his family came to the main entrance of the national park.

"I have my camera ready," his sister Marie said. "Nobody at school believed me when I told them what we saw the last time we were here."

During a talk around a campfire on the first night of their earlier visit, a ranger had described where to go to see wildlife, especially a herd of elk that had just moved into the park. The next day, they had seen them grazing on the budding plants. They were the largest animals Dominic and Marie had ever seen outside a zoo.

They decided then to come back later in the year to see the elk again.

By the time they could return, the leaves had already changed color and fallen off the trees. They drove to the meadow where they had seen the elk on their earlier visit, and although they drove all around, they could not see any this time. They stopped when they saw a ranger getting ready to lead a nature walk.

"Let's ask this ranger where the elk are. I hope they didn't all get killed by hunters," their father said as they got out of the car.

"I guess they could just be hiding," their mother suggested.

"But why would they? They were out in the open before," Marie said. "Maybe there was a disease? Or maybe wolves attacked them?"

Dominic said, "I think I might know what happened!"

"The elk migrated, didn't they?" Dominic asked the ranger. "The last time we were here was in the spring when the plants were budding and the elk had just come here from where they had spent the winter. But now it's late fall and I think they've left already."

"That's right," the ranger said. "Many creatures besides birds travel long distances each year with the changing of the seasons—some butterflies, sea turtles, and even bats migrate, just to name a few. The elk move to where there is a better supply of food and a less harsh climate for the winter. They will come back in the spring and I hope you will come back to see them then."

9

Egging Him On

"Is it a bird? Maybe it's a plane!" Woo-jin sang out.

"Cut it out, Woo-jin," his friend Grant retorted.

The boys had been walking through a field by a stream in a nature reserve when they came across some egg shells. Woo-jin was convinced that the egg shells were from birds, and he was running around flapping his wings in delight about his find.

While he let his friend frolic, Grant searched around the area, looking for nests.

"I don't think these eggs are from birds," he said as Woo-jin settled down and rejoined him. "For one thing, we're out in the open here and there are no trees."

"Wait, don't some birds build their nests on the ground?" Woo-jin asked. "I think I read once that turkeys do that. I guess they're too big and heavy to build nests in trees. Maybe these are turkey eggs, although they do look a little small for that. Maybe it's some smaller kind of bird," Woo-jin wondered.

Grant picked up one of the egg shells, feeling a soft and leathery cover.

"Actually, Woo-jin, I think we should leave," he said.

"What do you mean, Grant? Those are just empty shells. Why should we leave?" Woo-jin asked.

"I don't think these are bird shells at all. The way they feel, it makes me think they could be snake eggs," Grant said.

"Snakes?" Woo-jin said, jumping back.

"Well, maybe just turtles," Grant said. "Both turtles and snakes lay soft, leathery eggs, and both lay their eggs on the ground. I think we should to go to the nature center and show them these shells. I'm sure they'll know what laid the eggs."

One Good Turn

10

"Before we go, tell me, where do you hide your diary?" Katherine asked her best friend Seneca as they sat on the bed in Katherine's room.

"Under my bed with the key, nobody looks there anyway. Why, where do you hide yours?" Seneca replied.

"Well, my diary is under my bed too, but the key to it is under the plant!" Katherine whispered.

"That plant on the windowsill?" Seneca whispered back.

"Yes, but shhh, don't tell Lauren. She looks through all my stuff. I don't think she's read my diary yet, though," Katherine said about her little sister.

Katherine tipped the plant to show Seneca the key, careful not to disturb the leaves that were facing the window.

Soon afterward Lauren came in the room. "What are you guys doing?" she asked.

"Just getting ready to go to the ice cream store down the street," Katherine said as she got up. "Want to come along?"

"No, thanks," Lauren replied and left the room.

When Katherine and Seneca returned, they went back into Katherine's room and noticed the plant. The leaves seemed to reach out to the girls as they walked through the doorway.

"Katherine, I think Lauren has started reading your diary!" Seneca exclaimed.

"How do you know?" Katherine asked.

Seneca pointed to the leaves facing towards them. "This plant must have been moved," she said. "The leaves are pointed away from the sunlight coming through the window. Earlier, the leaves were facing the window, which is normal. It is due to phototropism, the term for plants that grow toward light, their source of energy. I think Lauren has been peeking at your diary. She must have moved the plant to get to the key, but didn't put the plant back exactly the way it was."

Horsing Around

Scott thought the large pond fed by a stream that came down off the mountain was one of the best parts of living in their town. In the winter, it would freeze over and there would be ice skating. During the rest of the year, he loved to fish.

At the start of fishing season each year, there was a family fishing day where families would pay a fee to join and receive cash prizes for different age groups. It brought the town together, made money to take care of the pond and was fun, all at the same time.

After Scott and his dad paid their fee, they carried the fishing equipment and bait to join others along the shore.

"Daddy, can you read me that sign?" Scott's little sister Emily asked.

"It says: $1 for catching a sunfish, $2 for catching a trout, $3 for catching a catfish, $500 for catching a seahorse," their father replied.

"Wow, $500!" she yelled.

"Don't get your hopes up," Scott said.

"Well, there are lots of other people fishing too," Emily said. "But we have as good a chance as anybody, don't we?"

"As bad a chance as anybody would be a better way to put it," Scott said.

She thought for a moment. "Do you mean it would be too small to catch with these hooks?" she asked. "Or are there hardly any seahorses in the pond?"

"The sign is a joke, just part of the fun," Scott explained. "There are no seahorses in the pond. Seahorses are warm water fish and they are native to salt water. This pond is fresh water and it gets too cold here for them even if this were salt water. Sorry, you're not going to catch one here!"

Life Line

"I wonder if Peanut is still here," Grandma said as she, Elena and Joseph walked into the zoo. She had joined them and their parents on a vacation to the city where she had gone to college years ago. One day, she offered to take the kids to the zoo so their parents could go out with some friends.

"Who's Peanut?" asked Joseph.

"An animal. I'll show you, if she's still here," Grandma said.

"How would you know an animal here by name?" Elena asked.

"I came to this zoo a lot when I was a college student," Grandma said. "Since I studied biology and zoology in school, my classes did research here. And I worked here during the summers. I got to know some of the animals very well."

"But you went to college a long time ago," Joseph said.

"Forty years ago," Grandma said. "I unfortunately lost touch with this place over the years."

"So there is no way that any animals from then are still here," Joseph protested.

"You don't think so?" Grandma asked.

"Some animals have very long life expectancies," Elena said. "Elephants, tortoises and some birds might have lived all this time."

Grandma nodded and said, "Elephants can live for more than 60 years. Tortoises and turtles can live to be at least 100 and birds such as macaws and parrots can also live more than 60 years. Some of those animals from 40 years ago could still be here."

"Okay, let's go," Joseph said. "If we're looking for an animal named Peanut, let's try the elephant house first."

Order in the Courtyard

When a new wing was added onto the back of the school, they made room for a courtyard. A school fair had raised money to turn the courtyard into a green area full of trees and shrubs native to the state. Students were allowed to take their lunches into the courtyard and eat at picnic tables while enjoying nature.

The small pond in the center of the courtyard was generally considered the best place to hang out. Once the water and plants were ready, it had been stocked with wildlife. The students especially enjoyed trying to find the turtles, which liked to hide under the bushes.

Jayla and Carly had finished eating lunch one day and were watching something swim around when Andre joined them.

"Found a minnow?" he asked.

"I don't think they put any fish in the pond, just frogs and turtles. This must be a young frog," Jayla said.

"Come on. Everybody knows the difference between a frog and a fish," Andre said. "This thing is shaped like a fish. It has gills and fins, and it lives underwater. That makes it a fish."

"She's right," Carly said. "Mr. Jenkins told me they didn't put any fish in the water. This must be a frog."

"Prove it," he said.

"I can, but you'll have to be patient," Jayla said.

"What do you mean?" he asked.

"Wait a month or so," Jayla said. "Frogs start as eggs, which hatch as tadpoles. At first, tadpoles look like fish and live underwater. As they grow, their tails and fins shrink, legs develop, lungs replace gills and eventually they can live on land. It takes about three months from when the egg was laid, and this tadpole is only about halfway through its metamorphosis."

Put Your Back Into It

"If I grow bean plants one more time, I'll go crazy," Dennis said as he walked home from school on a Friday with his friends Louis and Tristen.

At the end of their last period class, they had received information sheets about the upcoming science fair. They had to turn in their ideas on Monday morning. The past several years, the three of them had done group projects on growth of bean plants with different amounts of water, light and fertilizer. This year, they were supposed to do experiments on their own.

"I might do something with my sister's hermit crabs," Tristen mused. "Maybe I'll see if they prefer different levels of light."

"I've always liked that Pavlov's Dog thing," Louis said. "Maybe I'll see if I can train our dog Matey to do different tricks by ringing different kinds of bells."

"I might see if our hamsters can learn a maze," Dennis said. "I could build one with my dad."

"Hold on," Tristen said, looking at the instructions more closely. "It says we can't do an experiment with a vertebrate, not even a harmless experiment."

Dennis groaned. "It's back to growing bean plants for all of us," he said.

"Are you sure?" Tristen asked, disappointed.

"Dogs and hamsters have backbones, making them vertebrates," Louis said. "Sorry, Dennis. You and I have to come up with something else. But Tristen, you can use your idea for experimenting with hermit crabs. They have an exoskeleton—a skeleton outside the body. And creatures with exoskeletons are invertebrates."

"Alright!" Tristen said. "I'm sure you guys can find some other experiment to do that's better than growing beans."

15

Sweating It Out

It was another hot summer day. Garret had walked his family's lazy dog, Jessica, that morning and it had been his brother James's turn that afternoon since their parents were out grocery shopping. While James and Jessica were gone, Garret was in his room working on his summer math packet.

When he heard the front door open, Garret had come downstairs to see who was home, but only saw Jessica, who was all wet. She shook herself off, spraying water everywhere, then walked to her favorite spot and plopped herself down heavily, ready for a nap. Soon after, Garret heard the front door open again.

When James walked into the kitchen, he too was dripping wet.

"Why are you both so wet, James?" Garret asked.

"Jessica's just sweaty from her walk. I'm this wet because I went back out afterwards and jumped in the sprinkler to cool off," James answered. "Man, she sure sweats a lot."

Garret got a clean dish towel to dry Jessica off. As he did, he could feel she was taking regular breaths. She yawned.

"James, I know you didn't walk her," he said. "Now go walk her before Mom and Dad get home and we both get in trouble."

"What makes you think I didn't walk her?" James asked.

"Dogs don't sweat—at least, if they do, it's only a little bit through their footpads. Instead, they pant to cool off, so this water on her fur must be from the sprinkler," Garret said.

"Well, maybe I did walk her and just took her in the sprinkler with me at the end when we got home. Did you think of that?" James responded.

"I did. But it couldn't have happened that way, because of the way she's breathing," Garret said. "If she'd just been out for a walk on a hot day like this, she'd be panting, but she's not."

Earth and Space Science

16

It's All Alien to Me

Miss Vaughn divided her creative arts class into groups of four. Each student was to draw a scene of what one part of life might be like on another planet. Later, they would put them on poster board.

Kathleen's assignment was to show life inside an alien home. She drew the inside of the house with strange-looking gadgets and little green pets everywhere.

Joaquin's part was to show aliens at work. He drew a factory where robots were doing all the actual work and the aliens were just pushing buttons.

Albert's drawing showed aliens in school, wearing helmets that piped facts into their heads.

Valerie's part was to show recreation. She loved ice hockey, so her drawing had aliens wearing orange jerseys playing ice hockey on a pond.

"Now we just have to decide which planet this should be," Joaquin said as they arranged their pieces.

Miss Vaughn came to their group of desks and looked at the drawings. She said, "All the planets are taken except for Venus and Mars. Label yours with the one that fits all of your drawings better out of those two."

"What difference does it make which planet we choose?" Kathleen asked after Miss Vaughn left.

Albert said, "The inside scenes of home, work and school could fit on either planet since you control the environment inside a building. But we have to choose the planet with the outdoor environment that matches Valerie's pond scene."

"We can't pick Venus because it's so close to the Sun that it's too hot for ice," Valerie said. "But there is ice on Mars in its polar ice caps. So let's say this is life on Mars."

17

Where in the World?

As much as Leila missed having Chloe around for their summer vacation, she had to admit that Chloe must be having a great time traveling.

Chloe's father was working on a trade treaty between the United States and other countries bordering the Pacific Ocean. Since he would be traveling for weeks, he was allowed to take his family as long as he paid for them. Chloe and her mother would sightsee while her father worked. Every day Leila checked for a new e-mail from Chloe describing her adventures.

Chloe had given Leila the list of countries her family was visiting and so far they had been to four—with Japan, China and New Zealand still to go. But Chloe hadn't told Leila in what order they were visiting the countries. Instead, each time Chloe arrived in a new country she took pictures, attached them to an e-mail, and challenged Leila to figure out where she was.

This day's e-mail didn't have a picture, just a message: "We flew to a new country yesterday, but it got dark so early I couldn't take any pictures outside. I'll take some today and send them for you to guess what country it is."

Leila wrote back, "Send the pictures, but I already know where you are."

Later, a message came back from Chloe: "How do you know?"

"You must be in New Zealand," Leila wrote back. "That's the only country in the Southern Hemisphere out of the three still on the list. It's summer here in the Northern Hemisphere and the days stay light a long time, but it's winter there, meaning the Sun is up for a shorter time. It's due to the tilt of the Earth's axis, which causes light to shine longer on one hemisphere or the other at different times of the year as the Earth orbits the Sun. If it got dark early at this time of year where you are, you couldn't be in China or Japan, which are in the Northern Hemisphere."

18

Up in the Air

"I'm surprised at how hot it is here," Rylee and Aiden's father said as they settled onto a shaded picnic table.

They were on a trip through the Western mountain states and had just arrived that morning in Yellowstone National Park. They were having lunch while waiting for the next eruption of Old Faithful, which a ranger said was going to be in about half an hour.

"I'm afraid our hotel doesn't have a swimming pool," their mother said as she put water bottles on napkins that were about to blow away.

"Maybe we could take a walk in the woods later on," Rylee said. "It should be cooler in the trees."

Aiden was studying a map. "Look at this, there's a trail from here that goes past a lot of geysers. Not right next to them, but close."

"So?" Rylee said.

"So, we just follow that trail and we'll cool down," he said.

"But the trail is in the direct sunlight," she said, looking at the map.

"Aren't you forgetting the wind is blowing?" he asked.

"Aren't you forgetting something else?" she challenged.

"I'll bet you're thinking that because the path is so close to the geysers, the wind will blow a spray of water on us," Rylee said.

"Right," he said. "That will cool us down."

"But the water from a geyser is hot," she said. "The water under the ground gets heated to boiling by hot rocks. When the steam builds up enough pressure, it shoots out through a passageway to the surface. That's what makes a geyser. The last thing we want on a hot day is to be sprayed with hot water."

A Good Look

"I can always use extra credit," Noah said to himself as his teacher Mr. O'Shea handed out a list of projects the students could do to improve their grades.

One of them gave a date and said: "Directly observe the eclipse and write a short description of the event and its cause."

Later Noah was discussing it with his friends Omar and Marcos.

"How does he know there's going to be an eclipse on that day?" Marcos asked.

"I think the places and dates where eclipses can be seen are figured out a long time before they happen," Omar said. "In fact, I think the exact times are even figured out."

Noah looked at the sheet. "It doesn't say what time, just the date," he said. "Maybe I won't be able to do this after all."

"I'm sure that you'll find out closer to the date," Marcos said. "What's the difference?"

"For a solar eclipse, I'd have to make sure I'm not doing anything else at that time of the day," Noah said. "If it's during a school day, maybe I won't get excused from class."

"I don't think that's going to be a problem," Omar said.

"Why not?" Noah asked.

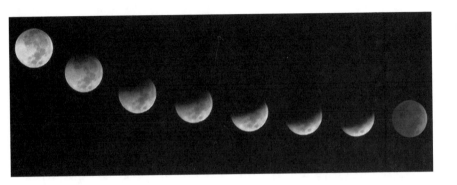

"It must be a lunar eclipse, not a solar eclipse," Omar said. "I'm sure Mr. O'Shea would never tell anyone to look directly at a solar eclipse. A solar eclipse happens when the Moon blocks out the Sun, but light from the Sun still shines around the edges and it will damage your eyes. In a lunar eclipse, the Earth comes between the Sun and the Moon, and the Earth's shadow falls over the Moon, turning it darker. A lunar eclipse is safe to look at, but a solar eclipse isn't. And lunar eclipses only happen at night, so you don't have to worry about getting out of class to see it."

Take a Hike

The students were pleased with the weather on the day of their field trip. It had rained the previous day and night, but this morning it was only cool and cloudy as the kids walked to the visitors center.

The class was learning about different ecosystems, and had taken a bus to a park with a meadow, a pond and woods. They were divided into three groups to collect samples and take pictures. They had walkie-talkies to keep in touch because cell phones didn't work there.

One group walked down a long, steep path to Frog Pond with Mr. Wysor. Marcel and Tucker's group hiked across to the meadow with Ms. Smith while the third group took on the task of studying the woods on a hillside with Mrs. Hammerick.

After an hour or so, Ms. Smith's group was finished. They walked back to the visitors center, but neither of the other groups had returned. Ms. Smith asked Marcel to check on them.

"We're finished in the meadow and can leave any time. How are you guys doing? Over," he said into the walkie-talkie.

"We have our samples and are just taking the last of the pictures. We will start walking back in a couple of minutes. Over," a voice replied.

"We're getting samples, but it's so foggy here the pictures won't be any good. Give us another 20 minutes. Maybe the fog will lift. Over," another voice responded.

"I didn't recognize those voices. Which group needs more time?" Tucker asked Marcel.

"It must be Mr. Wysor's group at Frog Pond that isn't finished yet," Marcel said. "Fog is more likely to form in low, damp areas, such as around a pond, especially when the ground is soaked like it would be from all that rain yesterday and the air is cool. Fog occurs when air cannot hold all the water vapor it contains and the vapor condenses into water droplets. So the group down at the pond must be who we are waiting for."

Think Green, Guys!

Pranav and Maneet's family had decided to buy a house in a new development. There were several models to pick from and they had chosen one with the features they wanted.

Two houses of that model were finished and were for sale. Their backs faced each other, one house looking north and the other looking south—each with a big, open lawn in front. There were tall trees between them, coming almost to the back of each house.

"It's hard to pick. These two houses are exactly the same," their mother said as they stood on the back deck of the house that faced north.

"The price is the same, too, although either way we're going to have to watch our money more closely after buying a new house," said their father.

Pranav could feel warmth in the sunlight even through the bare branches of the trees. Spring was coming. Where they lived, winter was short and mild and furnaces ran only a little. But summer was long and hot—air conditioners ran almost all day.

"We should buy this one," Pranav said after thinking for a moment.

"What did you do, flip a coin in your head?" Maneet asked.

"No, I was thinking about energy," Pranav said. "Everyone knows that the Sun appears to move from the eastern sky to the western sky, due to the Earth's rotation. But lots of people don't think about the other set of directions: north and south. For places north of the Tropic of Cancer, meaning every state except for Hawaii, the sun is always in the southern half of the sky. The trees are on the southern side of this northern-facing house, and on the northern side of that southern-facing house. Because the sun will be hitting both houses from the south, this house on the north will be shaded by the trees, while the house on the south won't be protected from the sun. This house won't absorb as much light energy from the sun, and it will stay cooler, so we won't have to run the air conditioning as much. We will reduce our use of electricity, saving money and the environment!"

Soil Solution

22

Reese was helping her father clean up the leaves and twigs that had fallen over the winter. It was time to get the yard and garden in shape for spring. Later, they would go to the garden store, but first they had to see what they needed.

At the side of the house, where a rainspout emptied out, they noticed that the grass had died, leaving bare dirt.

"We're going to have a problem with erosion this summer if we don't do something about this," her father said. "Most of the rain we get is from those big thunderstorms and the water runs off so fast it can wash away the soil unless the grass is strong enough. The worst of it is, except for those big storms, many years it's so dry that we have water restrictions."

There was a spigot and hose next to the garden but Reese remembered that the previous year there had been a ban against watering lawns or gardens. Their plants hadn't produced many vegetables.

"Maybe we can solve both problems at once," she said as they walked down the steep bank to the garden.

"Do you mean we should extend the downspout to the garden? The storms would just wash away the garden soil. Wouldn't that make things worse?" her father asked.

"No, I have a better idea," Reese said.

"What's that?"

"My idea is to have the downspout empty into a rain barrel," Reese said. "It would capture water from the storms so the soil won't erode. We'll get one of those barrels with a spigot on the bottom and run a hose from the barrel down to the garden. That way, we can water our garden even if there are water restrictions."

23

Make a Wish

"Now, this is what the sky should look like," Darnell said to Isaac as they sat on the porch of their grandparents' house in the mountains.

They were miles from even the nearest small town. It was perfectly quiet except for the chirping and buzzing of insects. They had never seen so many stars.

"Let's count the stars," Isaac said. "Has anyone ever tried that?"

"You can start, but you'll never finish," Darnell said, going inside to get a glass of water. When he returned, Isaac said, "I'll bet you a week of cleaning up after dinner that I know how many stars there are."

"You're on. How many are there?" Darnell said.

"One less than there was before you went inside," Isaac said triumphantly. "When you were in there, I saw a shooting star. I never promised to give you an exact number."

Darnell frowned. It was true, he hadn't asked for an exact number in the bet. "So, how is that one less star?" he asked.

"Because shooting stars burn up in the atmosphere," Isaac said. "Meaning now there's one less."

"Are you sure you want to keep that bet?" Darnell asked.

"Of course I'm sure. Why shouldn't I?"

"A 'shooting star' isn't a star," Darnell said. "Many of them are meteorites, which are rocks from space that enter the Earth's atmosphere. They heat up and melt away as they fall, causing streaks of light that people call shooting stars or falling stars. Sometimes a broken-off piece from a space ship or satellite that falls out of orbit does the same thing. If a real star ever got that close to Earth, it would be the Earth that burned up. So, there's the same number of stars as before I went inside."

Don't Rain On My Parade

"Don't forget extra socks," Jamal's father called up the stairs as Jamal was packing his soccer bag in his bedroom.

It was early Saturday morning. Soon they would be leaving for a round-robin tournament. There would be games starting in late morning and then all through the afternoon and into the early evening. For Jamal, it would mean a lot of running. For his parents and little sister Julissa it would mean a lot of sitting in folding chairs and finding something to do between games.

"I have books and magazines for us, and toys and coloring books for Julissa," their mother said from downstairs. "Should we pack umbrellas and rain ponchos?"

"I asked Julissa to watch the morning news for the weather report," their father replied.

Jamal thought Julissa might be a little too young for that chore but he was so busy packing that he didn't think much about it.

When they gathered by the front door Julissa reported proudly, "The lady on TV said there would be nothing but serious clouds all day."

"Serious clouds?" their mother asked. "I guess we should bring the rain gear, then."

"I wouldn't bother," Jamal said.

"Well, the games go on even if it rains, unless there's lightning," their father said. "So you'll have to accept getting wet. But what's the point in the rest of us getting soaked?"

"I meant that I don't think it will rain at all today," Jamal replied.

"You don't think 'serious clouds' suggest rain?"

Jamal said, "The word Julissa thought was 'serious' was likely 'cirrus.' Cirrus clouds are those high, thin clouds. They don't bring rain. Clouds that bring rain are lower and heavier—like nimbostratus clouds, which look like a thick blanket, or cumulonimbus clouds, which are the thick clouds that often come with thunderstorms. A day with nothing but cirrus clouds will not have rain."

Ship Shape

"Ahoy, mate!" Liam yelled, running into his older brother Theo's bedroom.

"Go back to bed," Theo growled. "It's six o'clock in the morning! I need my sleep, you know."

"But, Theo, there's part of a shipwreck out in the ocean! It looks like it's been there for a hundred years!"

"Then it will still be there when I get up," Theo grumbled and rolled over.

It was their family's first morning of vacation after arriving late the night before at a beach they'd never been to before. Liam was an early riser and had walked down to the beach just after dawn. Since Theo didn't want to get up and no one else was awake, Liam went to his room to read.

When Theo woke up around noon and went to the beach where his parents already had set up chairs and blankets, he saw sunburned people under umbrellas and sand crabs scurrying around, but nothing in the ocean except waves.

"Have you seen a shipwreck out there?" Theo asked his parents.

"No, but we've only been here for an hour," their father said to Theo. "We slept in a little. Then the three of us went straight to the grocery store while you slept."

"After we put away the groceries we came here," their mother added. "Liam told us about a shipwreck, but we haven't seen it yet."

"The shipwreck is out there and I'll prove it," Liam said.

"How?" Theo asked.

"We just have to look for it about six hours from now," Liam said. "I must have seen the shipwreck at low tide. Tides are caused by the gravitational pull of the Moon and are related to its orbit. A high tide comes about six hours after a low tide, and the next low tide comes about six hours after that. By the time Mom and Dad got here, the tide already was high enough to cover the shipwreck. If we look around six o'clock tonight, we should be able to see it."

Ups and Downs

Counselors-in-training, Darla and Cheyenne, were helping get the camp set up for the summer the week before it opened. That morning the head counselor Desirée had led them up the hill from the cabin area to an old campfire circle.

"I've got a job for you," Desirée said. "The camp wants to build a new campfire circle closer to the cabins. They're not going to use this one anymore, or the one down at the bottom of the hill. You can use the rocks from either place to build the new one."

"But rocks this big would be way too heavy to carry," Darla said.

"Get a wheelbarrow from the equipment shed," Desirée replied. "These rocks are just sitting loose on the ground. You can roll them right into the wheelbarrow."

Cheyenne and Darla walked down the hill. Getting from the top campfire circle to the cabin area on the hillside was a longer walk than going from the cabins to the lower campfire circle.

When they got the wheelbarrow, Cheyenne said, "Let's think for a minute. Where do we want to get the rocks?"

"Well, the rocks in both places are about the same size and they would weigh about the same," Darla observed.

"And it's a shorter distance from the lower campfire circle up to the cabins than it is from the upper circle down to the cabins," Cheyenne added. "So we should get the rocks from the lower circle. We won't have to push them as far that way."

"I'm not sure that makes sense," Darla replied.

"If we take the rocks from the lower circle, we'd be pushing a wheelbarrow full of rocks up the hill," Darla continued. "Gravity would be working against us. That's the force that attracts objects together, in this case pulling the rocks down the hill, closer to the center of the Earth. It will be much easier to bring the rocks down the hill, and let gravity work for us. Pushing an empty wheelbarrow up the hill for a longer distance is actually less work than pushing a full wheelbarrow up the hill for a shorter distance."

Room for More?

When the renovations to their house were finished, Drew's parents threw a party for their family and friends. Drew showed everyone his new room, which was larger than his old one.

The room looked even bigger because Drew liked everything neat and precise. Clothes were kept in closets and dressers, and books were on the bookshelves arranged by topic and size. A table in the corner held his chemistry set and microscope.

Some guests brought housewarming gifts, including a model of the solar system for Drew to paint and hang from his ceiling, since he liked science so much. When he finished setting it up several days later, he invited his parents in to come and look at it.

"Whoa, I better not get too close to the Sun. I could get burned," his father joked as he entered. A volleyball-sized Sun was hanging over his head.

"Let's see, that would be Mercury, Venus, Earth, Mars, Jupiter, Saturn, Uranus, Neptune," his mother said, looking down the line of planets ranging from a baseball-sized Jupiter to a golf ball-sized Mercury.

"Wouldn't it be great to have an exact model of the solar system?" Drew said.

"What's wrong with the one you have?" his father asked.

"It's the scale," Drew said. "The largest planet, Jupiter, has a diameter—that is, the distance across—almost thirty times bigger than the smallest, Mercury. The Sun has a diameter of nearly ten times that of Jupiter. That's much greater than the difference shown in this model."

"I see what you mean," his father said. "They would need to be a lot farther apart, too."

"We did a project on that at school," Drew said. "With a Sun about the size of this model, it was 30 feet just to get to Mercury, the first planet. Neptune would have been nearly half a mile away."

"Well, I don't think we'll be expanding this house again anytime soon, at least not by that much," his mother laughed.

Sundae Skies

"Finally, a good night to lie outside," Kiernan said.

The campers lay in a field waiting for the announcement to go back to their cabins for lights-out.

"It will be time to go inside soon," Mataya said. "It's completely dark now."

"I don't think I could move even if a bear came charging at me," Christine said, holding her stomach.

"I know what you mean. If I eat any more ice cream, I'm going to turn into a sundae," Kiernan said.

It had been a hot, tiring day and their stomachs were full. The camp had a rule that if the temperature was above 90 degrees by noon, the campers could have ice cream at each break time and meal to cool them off. Most over-did it by having ice cream several times, even though the temperature reached only a little above 90 all day.

The previous afternoon the sky had clouded over and it remained cloudy through that night and through the day. But around dinnertime the clouds had drifted away to let the girls gaze at sparkling stars and a full Moon before bed.

"Well, at least we had today to enjoy it," Mataya said. "I doubt we'll have unlimited ice cream tomorrow."

"Why not?" Christine asked. "It's as warm now as it was at this time last night."

"The cloudy sky last night helped trap in the heat radiating off the Earth," Mataya said. "That's why it was hot so early today. Tonight the sky is clear and the heat will radiate away into space. Tomorrow morning will be cooler. Since the temperature barely got above 90 by noon today, even with the trapped heat this morning, it probably won't get that hot by noon tomorrow."

On Top of the World

The fifth graders were setting up the auditorium for their promotion party, which was going to have an outer space theme. They would be in middle school next year. During the last several weeks after class, the students had made cutout stars, planets and spaceships to hang around the auditorium. Music from space movies would be playing as the principal handed out their certificates.

Nora was part of the group hanging decorations on the stage curtain. To one side was a large cutout of the Sun. Nora was hanging the Earth with Antarctica at the top.

"Hey, if you do that they'll think we've forgotten everything they taught us and they'll keep us here another year," Ashlee said to her.

"What, you think we'd all fall off the Earth that way?" Nora asked.

"No, I know about gravity. But you've got the Earth upside down," Ashlee said.

"Don't you think this fits the theme better?" Nora asked.

"How?" Ashlee said.

Nora said, "We think of Antarctica as being at the bottom of the Earth because that's the way globes and maps are usually made, at least here in the Northern Hemisphere. If you are in space, though, you can look at the planet from any direction you want. There's no top or bottom. So, whether Antarctica is on top of the Earth or on the bottom depends on from where you're viewing it."

Clothes Call

The mystery field trip had been the talk of the class for days. The students had been told only that they would be in one of three groups going to different places. When they reached their destinations, they would take notes and later would write reports.

Since the trips needed parents to be chaperones, some students had overheard their parents talking. The word around the school was that one group would be going to a cave, another to a rainforest exhibit at a museum, and the other to a waterfall in a park.

The teacher kept up the mystery until the end, though. The day before the trip, the assignment sheets she handed out did not say where a student was going, only what kind of clothes to wear for the field trip.

"Mine says I'm supposed to wear light clothing," Soo said on the bus home that day.

"'Bring a warm jacket,'" Estrella read off her sheet. "That's all my sheet says about clothes."

"I'm supposed to bring a waterproof jacket," Genevieve said.

"That means we're going to three different places," Soo said. "I still wish I knew where I'm going. I guess we'll just find out tomorrow."

"Why wait that long?" Genevieve said. "We can figure it out right now."

"Okay, let's see," Estrella said. "It's damp in a rainforest, so that could be where I'm going, or where you are going, Genevieve. Both of us are supposed to wear jackets."

"I suppose the spray from a waterfall could be pretty cold, so I think that's where Estrella is going with a warm jacket," Soo said.

Genevieve shook her head.

"A rainforest is damp, but hot," Genevieve said. "There would be no need to wear a jacket inside a rainforest exhibit. So that's where Soo must be going, with light clothing. Estrella's sheet only says a warm jacket, not a warm, waterproof jacket, so they're not asking her to be prepared to get wet. The waterproof jacket must be for the waterfall, which must be where I'm going. The warm jacket means you're going to the cave, Estrella. The temperature is cool in caves."

Physical and
Chemical Science

A Half-Baked Idea

31

"Save room for more!" Evelyn told her family during dinner. "I am making cookies for dessert!"

Evelyn's family was vacationing at the beach, far from their home high in the mountains. She loved to bake, and she always used the same recipes, so she had them memorized. She decided that she wanted to bake a treat for her family while they were all together on vacation.

She had gone grocery shopping earlier that day with her mother to get the supplies she needed, so after dinner all she had to do was mix the ingredients and bake them like always.

When she took the cookies out of the oven, she was appalled by what she saw. The cookies had all run together and still had not risen like they were supposed to. They looked really gross: half-burnt and half-baked.

When her older brother George walked by and saw them, he didn't make her feel any better, scrunching his nose and giving them a thumbs-down.

"Ew. What is wrong with your cookies? Did you put too much butter in them or something?" he asked.

"No! I did everything exactly the same as I normally do."

"Then that must be the problem," he said.

"What do you mean?"

"The recipe you used to make the cookies was one designed for high elevations," George said, "but when you tried to make your cookies the same way down here at sea level, it didn't work quite right. You are used to baking where the elevation is higher and the air pressure is lower. At high elevations, water evaporates more easily and the leavening agents that make the dough rise, like baking powder and baking soda, work more effectively. Here, there is more air pressure to keep water from evaporating and gas from rising as easily, which is why your cookies came out so runny. The ingredients, temperature, and time that you cook them all need to be adjusted. Why don't we look up a recipe for making these cookies at sea level and make a fresh batch?"

32

True Colors

One sunny day, William, Ava and Riley were helping at a neighborhood beautification project. An empty lot had been cleaned up, soil had been brought in, and earlier that day trees and bushes had been planted. William's father was watering them with a hose.

A professional artist had sketched a mural of the city skyline and people were painting it in. The three friends were working on a section of the sky when the artist joined them.

"Looks great," she said. "I think it's missing something, though. Let's put a rainbow right here."

She sketched an arc to show where the rainbow should go, and then left.

"Before we start painting the rainbow, we should make sure the colors are right," Ava said. "People will know we painted it and we don't want to mess up."

William said, "Okay, there's a memory trick to the colors of a rainbow...which I don't remember."

"I can't remember, either," Ava said.

"Or me," Riley said. "And it would be too embarrassing to ask. We should know this."

"Well, if we don't know and we're not willing to ask, how will we ever find out?" Ava asked.

"We'll conduct an experiment," William said. William led them to his father and asked to use the hose for a moment. William sprayed a fine mist into the sunlight, forming a spectrum of colors.

"The water droplets cause the sunlight to break into the colors that make it up, the same as what happens in the sky when water droplets create the conditions for a rainbow," William said. "Let's see, that's red, orange, yellow, green, blue, indigo, violet."

"And that reminds me of the memory trick," Riley said. "Roy G. Biv."

Tennis, Anyone?

33

"Sorry I'm late. We had to spend 10 minutes scraping the ice off the car before we could get going," Ignacio said as he joined the tennis class.

He and his friend Deshi were taking Saturday morning lessons at the tennis club's indoor courts. They both enjoyed tennis and hoped to be a doubles team when they got to high school. This was the first lesson of the new session.

The previous evening, Ignacio and Deshi had played a match there against two other friends and Ignacio's mother drove them home. On the way out, she had stopped at the front desk and bought several new cans of balls that were required for the lessons. Deshi had closed the car trunk for her when she put them inside.

Deshi's father had bought balls of the same brand for him on the way in to the lesson that morning. Since they each had new balls of the same kind, they didn't bother to keep them separate as they hit to each other to warm up.

Some of the balls bounced normally, but others seemed dead.

"What is wrong with these balls?" Ignacio asked. "Maybe we should ask for our money back."

"Before we do that, let's set the dead balls aside for a while," Deshi said. "They might go back to normal."

"You don't think they are permanently messed up?" Ignacio asked.

Deshi said, "You left the balls in the trunk of your car overnight, didn't you? They got cold in there and lost some of their bounciness because they stiffened up. In other words, they lost elasticity when they got cold. Also, since air contracts when it gets cold, it would make the air pressure in the tennis balls lower, making them seem flat and less bouncy. When they get back to room temperature, they should be okay."

Flying High

Sam and Jeffrey's grandfather had been a pilot in the Air Force years ago. One of his favorite places to take them was the annual air show at a military base nearby.

There were old biplanes, planes from World War II, and modern jets doing stunts and precision flying. There were also parachute drops, hot air balloon rides and even a blimp.

Their grandfather had flown many kinds of planes and liked to tell Sam and Jeffrey about them.

As they pulled into the parking lot, they heard a loud bang.

"I hope there wasn't a plane crash," Sam said.

"I think it was a cannon. Maybe as a signal that the show is about to start," Jeffrey said.

Their grandfather laughed. "Cannons are the Army's department, not the Air Force's. And I wouldn't worry that a plane crashed," he said. "We'd be hearing sirens if that happened."

"Wait, I remember from last time," Jeffrey said. "The sound comes from a plane, but not from a crash."

"You mean it fired a missile?" Sam asked.

"What we heard was a sonic boom," Jeffrey said. "A jet must have flown over us going faster than the speed of sound."

"Which is about 760 miles an hour, although the exact speed can vary by temperature and for other reasons," their grandfather said. "What happens is that the air in front of the airplane gets compressed so much from the high speed of the plane that it creates a shock wave that sounds like an explosion—a sonic boom."

Eggcellent Idea

35

"Mom, where are you?" Carol called as she unlocked the back door and entered the kitchen.

Three other equally sweaty and hungry girls followed her after playing a pick-up soccer game on the field near Carol's house.

On the table, they saw a note from Carol's mother. It said, "Had to run an errand. Will be back around one. You and your friends can help yourself to lunch. Eggs are in the fridge."

"Mom boiled a dozen eggs this morning to make egg salad sandwiches. I know how to make them," Carol said as she opened the refrigerator.

Two identical egg cartons were inside.

"How do we know which dozen is hard-boiled?" Bianca asked. "If we crack one open and it's still raw, we're wasting an egg and making a mess."

"How about seeing if any are still warm?" Jade suggested. "Or still wet from being in the water?"

Carol brought out both egg containers and felt the eggs. All the eggs were cold and dry.

"That doesn't help. They're all the same. I think we have to guess," she said.

"We don't have to guess," Lucy said.

All their heads turned toward her.

Lucy explained, "Spin the eggs here on the counter. They will spin differently. The raw ones will spin more slowly than hard-boiled ones. That's because the hard-boiled eggs have been cooked solid, but the liquid inside of the raw egg will slow the egg down. That's how we will be able to tell which eggs are which."

A Girl's Best Friend

36

"Happy birthday to you," Samara's friends ended the song in the lunchroom as she turned red from embarrassment.

Samara had brought cupcakes for homeroom that morning, and now was giving the last ones to the girls she ate lunch with every day, Natalia and Violet.

"Hey, what's with the two necklaces?" Violet asked. She noticed for the first time that Samara was wearing her usual necklace of wooden beads and also one Violet hadn't seen before with a small, shiny clear stone dangling on a silver chain.

"My parents gave it to me last night. It's my birthstone," Samara said. "A diamond for April."

"Wow, a real diamond? You have to take good care of that," Natalia said.

"I'm only going to wear it to special places, not every day. I only wore it today to show you guys," Samara said. "But this is a strong necklace, so I'm not worried about the stone falling off."

"I was thinking about the diamond getting scratched by rubbing against your other necklace," Violet said.

"I don't think she has to worry about that," Natalia said.

"Why not?" Violet asked.

Mohs Scale of Mineral Hardness

Mohs hardness	Mineral	Chemical formula	Absolute hardness	Image
1	Talc	$Mg_3Si_4O_{10}(OH)_2$	1	
5	Apatite	$Ca_5(PO_4)_3(OH-,Cl-,F-)$	48	
7	Quartz	SiO_2	100	
9	Corundum	Al_2O_3	400	
10	Diamond	C	1600	

"Because a diamond is one of the hardest substances there is," Samara said. "Remember that 10-level scale of mineral hardness from science class? It's called Mohs Scale. Diamonds are at the top. The diamond might get a little dirty rubbing against the wooden beads, but it won't get scratched."

37

Tea Trouble for Two

Olivia's mother opened the apartment door carrying groceries, and Olivia helped take them into the kitchen. Her younger brother Austin joined them and started to unload the bags, but he stopped when he saw their mother had bought him the latest edition of his favorite comic book series.

Olivia noticed a box of tea different from the brand their mother usually used.

"I thought I'd try that kind, it looked good," their mother said. "Austin, would you make me a cup of that tea while Olivia and I go down for the rest of the bags?"

They had to take the elevator to the parking garage, and the trip down and back up took a number of minutes.

When they returned, Austin had disappeared into his bedroom with the comic book. A cup of water was sitting on the counter with a teabag in it. The water had barely changed color. "I guess this brand of tea takes longer," their mother said, glancing at it.

They didn't touch it while they put away the groceries.

When they finished, the water still had barely changed color.

"I don't know if I'm going to like this brand of tea if it's so weak," their mother said.

"I wouldn't give up on it so soon," Olivia said.

"Do you mean I should wait even longer?"

"The problem may be the water, not the tea. Maybe Austin didn't get the water hot enough, or maybe he didn't heat it at all," Olivia said. "We haven't checked that. Heating something increases the motion of its molecules, which, in this case, causes the water molecules to extract more flavor and color from the tea leaves."

Her mother touched the cup. "You're right, it's cold. I'll have to teach Austin the right way to make tea."

38

Finding a Solution

Spring had turned the corner and twins Frances and Fiona were pleased that they could start spending time outside in the back yard. The family's yard was sheltered by trees with long braches, perfect for the girls' hobby of bird watching.

Frances had the job of mixing sugar in water for their hummingbird feeder. In the past, the girls noticed that more hummingbirds came to the feeder when they used a more sugary mix, so this year Frances had decided to make the mix as sweet as possible. In the kitchen, she added sugar to hot water until sugar started collecting in the bottom of the pot even though she was stirring it. Then she filled the feeder with the water.

"I just love it when we get to see so many hummingbirds!" Frances said as she screwed the lid onto the feeder.

The girls hung the feeder on a tree branch where they could watch from their deck. It took a few days for the hummingbirds to start coming. But when they did, the birds left almost instantly each time.

The girls went out to check the feeder.

"I think I see the problem," Fiona said, scraping powder from the feeding holes.

"Where did that come from?" Frances asked.

"The birds can't get the mix out of the feeder," Fiona said. "This powder clogging the holes is sugar."

"I didn't put any sugar on the outside," Frances protested. "And I stopped putting more sugar in the water when it started collecting at the bottom when I was stirring it. I know that when there's as much sugar as the water can hold, it's saturated, and it won't be able to dissolve anymore. Isn't that right?"

"Yes," Fiona said, "but hot water can hold more sugar than cool water—that is, the saturation point is higher when the water is hotter. Once the water cools, some of the sugar can't stay in solution and the sugar precipitates—it reforms into crystals and collects at the bottom. That sugar is blocking the sweetened water from getting out, so the hummingbirds leave. Let's clean it out and try again with less sugar."

Drafty Days

Stefan's mother came in the front door with his younger brother and sister, Nik and Teodora. She had brought them back from different parties and was carrying paper streamers she had loaned as decorations.

Nik had been at a season-end party for his T-ball team at a pizza restaurant that had a rack of free helium balloons on strings by the exit. Nik, of course, had taken one, as he always did and also brought home a goodie bag of candy and his team trophy.

Teodora, the youngest, had been at a birthday party. As part of her goodie bag, she had gotten a bright green kazoo and a feather boa, which was wrapped around her neck and already dropping feathers.

Meanwhile, Stefan and his father had gone to the hardware store to buy insulation and weather stripping. The weather had just turned colder and the house was feeling drafty and chilly.

"How's it going?" Stefan's mother asked.

"Well, we have the supplies we need," Stefan's father said. "But the problem is, we can't figure out where the draft is coming from. It could be from the windows, the chimney, the doors, or the attic steps. Or maybe all of them."

"Actually, Nik and Teodora just brought in something that will give us the answer," Stefan said.

"What we need is something light enough to show where there's just a slight movement of air, which is what a draft is," Stefan said. "Even a feather or a streamer probably would be too heavy. But a helium balloon is lighter than air. Let's take the balloon to all the places the draft might be coming from. Wherever it moves, we'll know there's air in motion."

Tricks with Bricks

Kyo, Kei and their father walked out of the house after lunch on a hot and sunny day and admired their work so far on their sidewalk project. They had spent the morning preparing the walkway in front of their house, making an even layer of gravel and sand.

The bricks had been delivered a few days before. The boys were excited to finally use them to build the new sidewalk. Their father had experience with bricklaying, and he was teaching them about it.

Half of the bricks were black, the other half white. They were going to make a pattern in the sidewalk, each boy taking one color.

Kei took several white bricks and arranged them in the first row along the straight line their father had strung across the walkway, while his younger brother Kyo watched. But just as Kyo was about to go get the first black bricks, their father stopped him and handed him a pair of work gloves.

The boys walked over to the bricks and Kyo put the gloves in his back pocket rather than wearing them. "Dad doesn't think I'm old enough or strong enough to do this with my bare hands," he whispered to Kei. "But I am."

As Kyo reached for the first brick, Kei said, "Hold on, that's not the reason he gave you the gloves."

"What was the reason then?" Kyo asked.

"The bricks have been sitting out in the sun all day," Kei said. "They are going to be way too hot to touch."

"But the white ones weren't too hot for you," Kyo retorted. "Why would the color make any difference?"

"Black objects absorb all visible light. That means they absorb more energy from sunlight than white objects, which reflect light rather than absorb it. That makes the black bricks hotter. Probably too hot to handle," Kei said.

Kyo put his hand above the black bricks, felt the heat radiating off them, and put on the gloves. "Thanks Kei!" Kyo said. "You just saved me from a bunch of blisters!"

The Tune-Up

Taryn played clarinet in her middle school band and was thinking about taking band as an elective course once she went to high school. Her older brother Seamus had done that. He was now in his first year playing trumpet in the high school band.

To help music students decide whether they wanted to be in the high school band, the middle school took them to watch the high school band prepare and then play at the football game one Friday evening.

It was the first cold day of the fall, so Taryn and her friends bundled up as they watched the game and the band show at halftime. After the game, she and her friend Fay went back to the band room, where the band members were putting away their instruments.

"That was a great show, Seamus," Fay said.

"The marching was good but the music seemed off to me," Seamus said. "The songs sounded so much better when we were practicing in here before the game."

"Were people missing their notes?" Fay asked.

"No, it wasn't that. Everyone hit the notes. It just didn't sound right," he said. "I wonder what happened?"

"The cold weather happened," Taryn said. "Your instruments were in tune here in this warm room, but when you were outside, they got cold and contracted slightly. That changed the vibrations the instruments produced and changed the sound a little bit. Then there's also the effect of the air temperature on the sound of the music. Everyone knows that light travels faster than sound, but not everyone knows that sound travels more slowly when the air temperature is colder, making it sound a little off. You have a good ear for music. A lot of people wouldn't even notice that."

Fire in the Hole

"This reminds me of that old saying: the difference between the right word and almost the right word is the difference between lightning and lightning bug," Xavier and Jocelyn's father said. Their father often used old sayings, especially when they were doing something he did as a kid—like now, when they were catching fireflies. Before, they had lived in a part of the country where there were no fireflies, but recently they had moved near where he grew up. He showed them how to hold out a hand and let the firefly land on it.

Their father brought out an empty jelly jar with a metal lid to put them in, but then remembered something. "They need holes in the lid," he said, going back inside the house. "I'll get a hammer and a nail to punch some out."

Xavier and Jocelyn watched the fireflies crawl around inside the jar, flashing their lights every few seconds. Xavier had to hold his hand over the opening to keep them inside.

"I guess he means that with all this flashing, they'll use up all the oxygen if we have a lid without holes," Jocelyn said. "Or maybe he thinks it will get too hot for them from the fire they're making?"

"It must be to give them air to breathe," Xavier said. "A firefly's light is not real fire. It's a reaction among chemicals in their bodies that produces light but not heat."

Statues on Wheels

Once the skateboard park opened, it became a favorite Saturday afternoon hangout for Moises and his friends. They had taken lessons and were preparing an exhibition for the parents at the end of the lesson series to show off their new skills.

Moises and Braylon were standing atop the highest wall, planning what they would do in the exhibition. Some of the routines would feature tricks, but theirs was supposed to show control and balance.

"My idea is that one of us starts here, and the other starts on the other side of the bowl," Braylon said, pointing to the lower wall on the other side. "We start at the same time, go straight across and pass close to each other. No other movement—no pushing off, no braking. It'll be like we're statues. Each of us will go to the top of the opposite wall and we'll do it again, same way, a couple more times, with a different statue pose each time."

"That will show a lot of balance and control. And I think it will work except for one part," Moises said.

"What's that?" Braylon asked.

"The person standing on the higher ledge at the start will have more potential energy than the person standing on the lower ledge," Moises said. "When we go off the ledges, that potential energy will change into kinetic energy. But the person starting on the lower wall won't have enough kinetic energy to make it to the top of the higher wall. Not without adding more kinetic energy by pushing off."

"You're right," Braylon said. "How about this? Whoever is on the lower wall will push himself off, adding energy, while whoever is on the higher wall will just pretend to push off, in order to make us look the same. It will take practice, but I'm sure we can do it."

Making Light of a Problem

Stephanie and her mother were walking around the gift shop at a ski resort they were visiting for the weekend. At more than 9,000 feet, it was nice and cool even in mid-summer. Stephanie was looking for a gift for her older brother, since his birthday was coming up. Finally, she decided on a lighter with a pretty picture of the Rocky Mountains on it.

"Hey Mom, do you think Patrick would like this lighter?" Stephanie asked.

"He would," her mother replied. "That would be really useful for all his camping trips. Just make sure it works before you buy it."

Stephanie had never used a lighter before, so she struggled to pull the roller and push the button at the same time. After a few tries, she finally managed to do both. A flame flickered briefly but didn't stay lit. She tried another lighter and then a third, with the same problem.

"Mom? Could you try this? It's not working for me," Stephanie said, frustrated.

Stephanie's mother also tried several lighters but got the same result. She went up to the cashier to tell him they were broken.

"The lighters work," the cashier answered. "They just don't work *here*."

"Wait! I think I know what's wrong!" Stephanie exclaimed.

"There's not enough oxygen at this high elevation," Stephanie explained, and the cashier nodded in agreement. "The atmosphere is thinner and there is less oxygen. You need oxygen to sustain a fire, which is why these lighters aren't working."

"We're almost two miles above sea level," the cashier said. "Another problem could be that they're too cold to work consistently. The lighters are often fickle when people try to get them to work up here, but I assure you they will work down at a lower elevation, especially once they warm up a little."

The Reverberating Roar

Colton was visiting his grandparents at their new home on a lake with his friend Max for the weekend. It was a quiet Saturday afternoon, but later some local bands were having a talent contest outside the community center at the far end of the lake.

"We'll go there later on," Colton's grandmother said as they arranged some chairs on their dock. "Our neighbor's son is in the third band and we promised we'd go hear him."

"Each band is playing a couple of songs," Colton's grandfather added. "I'm sure we'll be able to hear the first band from our side of the lake when the contest starts and we'll still have time to drive there."

Max and Colton swam, fished and explored the shoreline for a few hours. Later at the dock they started hearing low notes coming from the direction of the community center.

"The band contest has started," Colton said.

Colton's grandfather listened for a moment and said, "It sounds like just a bass player, practicing a song until the rest of the band is ready. We can wait until we hear the actual music start."

"Um, I think Colton is right," Max suggested.

"Can you see that far?" Colton's grandmother asked, squinting at the building just barely visible in the distance.

"Lower frequency sounds carry better over a distance than higher frequency sounds," Max said. "That's why we hear the bass player even though we can't hear the higher frequency sounds the other instruments and singers are making."

"What made you think of that?" Colton's grandfather asked.

"Actually, it was a field trip our class took to the zoo last year," Colton said. "The zookeeper said that elephants can communicate with each other miles apart, because they make low-pitched sounds. She said it works the same with whales."

General Science

46

Halloween Hippie

"Hey, I have an old picture of my grandma looking just like that, only it wasn't a costume to her," Kassandra said as Ingrid walked into the homeroom. "She said they actually thought they looked cool."

Their school normally had a dress code, but it was Halloween and everyone had come in that day wearing costumes. Ingrid was dressed like a hippie. She had a tie-dyed shirt, beads, sandals and sunglasses with orange lenses shaped like hearts.

Ingrid took off the sunglasses for class, but she put them back on when it was time to get ready for the Halloween party in the afternoon. The class was decorating the classroom and painting signs for the school parade.

Quan, who thought he was funny, was hanging decorations upside down; Preston was pretending to sword fight in his pirate costume with a paint brush and Ricky was playing with fake blood after putting some on his zombie costume.

When it was almost time for the parade, Kassandra noticed that one of the signs had been decorated with a red, rather than orange, pumpkin.

"Okay, who's the joker here?" Kassandra asked.

She looked around the room for a guilty face.

"I see now," Kassandra said. "It's your orange-colored sunglasses, Ingrid. They make everything look the same color to you. They're acting as filters so that light of only some colors come through to your eyes, but other colors are blocked. What you thought was orange paint is actually red. Take off those sunglasses and you'll see."

"Oops," Ingrid said, laughing. "I guess we'll just paint some flames on it and call it a pumpkin on fire!"

47

Weighting Game

"Row, row, row your boat," Antoine chuckled as he, Mikel and their cabin mates walked to the lake. It was the last full day of camp and they had prepared all week for the boat race of their cabin against another cabin of boys the same age. The boats would go from the dock, around a marker near the far end of the lake, and then back to the dock.

"Bad news, guys," a counselor named Nick said when the two groups reached the dock. He was holding the orange ball with a handle attached that was used as the floating marker.

"The rope that was holding this broke," Nick said. "I have a new rope, but now we need a new anchor to hold the marker in place. The pre-competition is to find something heavy that we can use as the anchor. The first team to come back here with something to use gets a two boat-length head start in the race."

Both teams dashed away to find something heavy. Antoine noticed the boys from the other team were going into the sports shed while his group was looking around the stable nearby.

A boy from the other cabin soon emerged from the shed carrying a bowling pin and their team started running back to the dock, laughing and cheering.

"Oh no!" Mikel said. "They found something really heavy before we did."

"Don't worry," Antoine smiled as he picked up a horseshoe.

"But they're already on their way!" Mikel said. "What can we do?"

"They may get there first, but we're going to get that head start in the boat race," Antoine said. "A bowling pin won't work as an anchor."

"But bowling pins are really heavy—heavier than a horseshoe for sure," Mikel said.

"It's not how much something weighs that determines whether it sinks in water; it's the density of the object compared with the density of water," Antoine said. "This horseshoe will sink because the density of the iron it's made of is higher than the density of water. A bowling pin is made of wood, which is less dense than water, so it will float."

48

Pooling Their Thoughts

Leo's older brother Zane had just started working as a lifeguard at their neighborhood pool. When the lifeguards weren't on duty in a chair or doing other jobs like working at the front desk, they went to their break room. It was a converted storage room down a hallway inside the bath house.

Leo knocked on the closed door and called, "Zane? Mom told me to bring you more suntan lotion. She says you look like a lobster."

"Come in," Zane said, opening the door. "Watch your step. Those floor tiles are always slippery."

Leo looked around. The room had some old chairs and a table where several lifeguards were eating pizza. A radio was playing, and towels and swimsuits were hanging on drying racks. But what Leo noticed most was how uncomfortable the air was.

"Wow, how can you stand it in here?" Leo asked.

"Yeah, it is pretty muggy," Zane said. "There's no air conditioning and no window to open or put an air conditioner in. And they make us keep the door closed so the music doesn't bother anyone. Still, it's the only place for us to hang out."

"I know what you could do to make it feel less sticky, at least," Leo said.

"You mean get a fan?" Zane asked.

"No, a fan won't solve the problem. The problem is that the humidity of the air is so high from all these wet towels and bathing suits," Leo said. "Warm air can hold more moisture than cooler air. It feels so sticky in here because your body doesn't cool itself as well—the moisture on your skin evaporates more slowly into air that's already holding so much water. A fan will just blow that damp air around. Since there's no window for an air conditioner, what you need is a dehumidifier."

Science Friction

One day Ms. Joni divided her science class into three groups to use what they were learning in both her class and writing class.

"Your assignment is to make a movie poster of a science fiction movie like they did years ago," she said. "Be creative and remember those movies had a lot of action and were scary. But the basic science has to be accurate."

After a few days of working, the groups put their posters in the front of the room. The students then would judge which one was the best—no voting for their own poster allowed. The winning group would be rewarded with no homework for the weekend.

One poster was titled "Insects Take Over the Earth!" It showed an army of ants, an air force of flying grasshoppers and a spider general leading them.

The second poster showed a submarine under a sheet of ice being attacked by a giant octopus. "Lost Under the South Pole and Fighting for Their Lives!" it said.

The last was called "The Weird World Where Birds Can't Fly, but Mammals Can!" It showed birds walking along the ground looking up at furry creatures flying overhead.

"I think we have the winner," said Roxanne, who was in the third group.

"I bet you don't," said Elliott, who was in the second group. "Ours is much scarier."

"And my group's poster has a lot more action," said Erwann, who was in the first group. "What makes you think you're going to win, Roxanne?"

"All the posters showed a lot of imagination, but only one met the science requirement," Roxanne said.

"There is water under the ice at the North Pole," she continued, "but there is ground under the ice at the South Pole—the continent of Antarctica. A submarine can't go under the South Pole, and an octopus wouldn't go there anyway, because they live in warm water."

"And spiders are not insects, they're arachnids—the easy way to remember is that insects have six legs and arachnids have eight," she added. "So it's not accurate to have a spider on a poster about insects."

"I see," Elliott said. "But there are birds that don't fly, such as penguins and ostriches. And bats are mammals that do fly. So at least the idea behind your poster is based in science."

To Catch a Chill

"I can't believe my mother made me wear this heavy coat," Paige complained as she walked to school with friends one morning.

"My mother is the same way," Tyra said, splashing through a puddle in her heavy waterproof boots.

"Hey, wait a minute," Lin said, picking up her hat as it had blown off her head. "Were your mothers listening to that new radio station all the parents like that plays those old songs?"

"Yes!" Paige said. "I can't believe the music they play!"

"Some of those songs must be 20 years old!" Tyra added.

"It was on at our house, too," Lin said. "I heard the announcer say that it would feel like 25 degrees this morning and that is when my mom handed me these gloves."

"So what?" Paige asked.

"I see what Lin means," Tyra said, jumping from puddle to puddle. "At 25 degrees Fahrenheit, this water would be frozen. Water freezes at 32 degrees and below."

"I think our parents should start listening to a different radio station," Lin said.

"I don't think that would help," Paige said.

"Why wouldn't it? The people at that station clearly don't know anything more about weather than they know about music," Tyra said.

"When the announcers said what the temperature would feel like, they were talking about the wind chill factor, not the air temperature," Paige said. "Even though the air isn't 25 degrees, this wind makes it feel like it is that cold. Wind chill is a measure of how cold it feels to us because the wind is blowing away the heat that our bodies make. Wind also causes faster evaporation of moisture from the skin which makes the skin feel cooler. So, the wind chill factor number can be below freezing even though the air temperature is above freezing."

Silver, Where?

The Thanksgiving meal had been baking all morning and it was now time to set the table. That was a job for Rubi and Mariana.

As a wedding present years ago, their grandparents had given their parents silverware they had bought many years before. They only used the silverware on special occasions like today and they always washed it by hand.

"Hugo, you need to get out of the way," Rubi said. Their little brother was sitting on the kitchen floor, making words on the refrigerator with letter magnets.

"Yes, we don't want to risk tripping and dropping one of the plates," Mariana said.

"Do you think this silverware really is made of pure silver?" Mariana asked as they set the table.

"I think pure silver is pretty rare. A lot of silverware has just a thin layer of silver over some other less expensive metal like steel," Rubi said. "Although I guess there's one way to check."

She looked at Hugo.

"Use his magnets?" Mariana said. "If there is a magnetic metal such as steel under the silver it'll definitely be magnetic. But silver is a metal too, so wouldn't it be magnetic whether or not there is a different metal underneath the silver?"

"Not all metals are magnetic, or at least are not magnetic enough to make an ordinary magnet stick to them," Rubi said. "Silver is one of those. Gold is another."

The magnets did not stick to the silverware. "Probably these really are pure silver," Mariana said. "But to be sure, we'd have to take them to an expert."

"By the way," Rubi added. "Even what is called a 'pure' silver utensil has a little bit of other metal mixed in with the silver. That's done to make the utensil harder, since silver is so soft. But in this case at least, it wasn't enough to make the utensil magnetic."

Court Code

"Closed for repairs: courts at high school are open," read the sign at the middle school outdoor basketball courts.

Brent and his little sister Bethany had arrived before their friends, Parker and Joanna, who were coming to play them in a game of two-on-two on a sunny Saturday morning.

The high school was up a hill from the middle school. When they arrived there, though, all the courts except one were being used.

"Sorry, because there are fewer courts available today, you can't take a court until all of your players are here," the attendant said. "Your friends better hurry because a group of high school boys is coming back soon. They drove off to pick up the rest of their players when I told them."

Looking down from the high school courts, they could see their friends walking toward the middle school.

"We need them to come straight here or we might not get the court," Brent said.

They yelled and waved their arms, but their friends didn't hear or see them and kept heading toward the middle school.

"Do you have your cell phone with you?" Bethany asked.

Brent pulled it out of his pocket and tried calling. "Oh no, the battery is dead," he said. "How can we get their attention? Do you have anything that might work?"

Bethany looked through her bag, and found a compact mirror her mother had given to her when she started middle school.

"Aha! We can just use this," she said triumphantly.

Brent looked confused. "How are you going to get their attention with that?" he asked.

Bethany held up the mirror and twisted it so that the sunlight glinted off of it. The flashes caught their friends' attention and they saw Brent and Bethany waving to them to come to the high school courts. Parker and Joanna got there just in time to start playing before the high school boys arrived.

"The sound of us yelling spread out and became too faint to hear at that distance but the light reflected off my mirror was visible at that distance. People used to use mirrors to signal like that way before cell phones were even invented," Bethany said.

Home on the Range

Guillermo and Fiorella's family was enjoying their last hike of the fall before the weather turned too cold to go hiking.

Halfway up a mountain on a trail they had never taken before, their father said, "This would be a great spot to have a house."

They looked around the edge of the sunny meadow, down to a stream, feeling a fresh breeze coming down the mountain.

"You're right, Dad," Guillermo said.

"I would love to live here, too," said Fiorella. "It's so pretty and I'm sure there are deer and all kinds of other animals here. It would be great to watch wildlife right from our front porch."

"I don't know about living in a place like this," their mother said. "There's no electricity and you kids couldn't live for more than a day without your gizmos. You could never get the power company to run an electrical line this far out into the woods."

"Well, if we were allowed to build a house here, we could make our own electricity," Fiorella said.

"But making electricity requires energy. Where would we get it?" their father asked.

"There is solar energy since the Sun shines directly on this meadow," Fiorella said.

"But what if the Sun isn't shining?" their mother challenged them.

"In that case, we could use the wind power," Guillermo said.

"And if the wind isn't blowing?" their father asked.

"There's running water. We could put up a water wheel," Fiorella said.

"And to stay warm, we could collect wood and burn it in a wood-burning stove, although that would create some air pollution from the smoke," Guillermo added.

"Too bad this is in a national forest and you can't build houses here," their father said, "Otherwise, I'd be tempted to try living here."

Time for a Change

Ivan's father had bought new smoke detectors six months earlier, putting one on each level of their house: one in the laundry room downstairs, one in the sunroom on the main level and one in the upstairs hall between the bedrooms. The smoke detectors sent wireless signals to an alarm system.

Ivan's father had asked him to replace the batteries and looked surprised when Ivan brought the smoke detectors to him where he was working at his tool bench in the garage. That was where they kept the fresh batteries.

"You didn't have to take them off their bases," his father said. "You could have just taken the new batteries, opened each smoke detector where it was, and switched the batteries there."

"Sorry, I guess I didn't understand what you meant," Ivan said. "Can't we just change them here?"

"We'll do that, but we have to put each smoke detector back in the same place or the alarm system won't work right," his father said. "And they're all the same, except that the color of one is more faded than the others and one has some dark spots."

"At least that tells us what we need to know, doesn't it?" Ivan asked.

"This faded one must be the one from the sunroom, the brightest of the three places," Ivan said, setting aside the one with the lighter color. "And the dark spots on this one are mildew, meaning it must have come from a damp, dark place—the laundry room. That leaves the other one for the upstairs hall."

55

Don't Let the Bugs Bite

"Man, these mosquitoes are eating me alive," Franklin complained, slapping at his arms and legs.

The neighborhood kids were playing volleyball in Franklin's back yard. His parents had recently bought the net and set it up, but it was hard to stay out in the yard long because of the mosquitoes. They would even bite people wearing mosquito repellant.

"Dad! Can you do something about these bugs?" Franklin called to his father, who was reading a book inside their screened-in porch.

Franklin's father came out to the yard and lit the citronella torches that were along the edge of the yard. There was a bucket of water next to each one.

"What are these buckets for?" Landon asked. Landon was new to the neighborhood and had never been to Franklin's house before.

"We put them here in case a torch falls, so nothing catches on fire. We just fill them at the beginning of the spring and leave them here all summer," Franklin said. "If they get a little low on water we just add some more."

"I hope this works," Franklin's father added as the torches started smoking. "Otherwise, we might have to hire one of those companies to spray the yard."

"Can I suggest something else?" Landon asked.

"This water might be a cause of the problem," Landon said. "Mosquitoes lay their eggs in water and the eggs need a week or so to hatch. Without water, the eggs don't hatch. These buckets should be emptied and refilled every couple of days. Adult mosquitoes only live a few weeks, so they should start dying out if you keep the eggs from hatching."

"Good idea," Franklin said. "And I'll make sure that water isn't collecting anywhere else, either."

A Floating Idea

56

One of the fun activities in town was to float in inner tubes at the local lazy river. Mr. Allen took his middle school class one day as a reward for good grades and behavior in class.

They loaded cars with their inner tubes and got there in no time. After an hour of floating, they had gone about a mile. Some parents would meet them farther downstream and drive them back.

"Hey, Mr. Allen, I think you're sinking," Whitney said as she floated behind him. "You're riding pretty low in the water."

"I wasn't paying attention, but you're right," he responded. "My inner tube must have a leak somewhere."

Mr. Allen paddled to the side and stood up. "I have a repair kit here in my backpack with a patch and an air pump, but first, I need to find the leak," he said.

The students all paddled over to him and got out of their inner tubes. After closely inspecting Mr. Allen's inner tube for several minutes, they couldn't find a hole.

"I guess I'll be walking part of the way," Mr. Allen said. "The rest of the air will leak out soon, and it won't help to pump more air in if it's just going to leak right out."

"I don't think that you should give up yet," Whitney said. "Everyone, come help me for a minute."

"What do you have in mind?" David asked. "All of us looked at it already."

Whitney said, "If we push it under the water, we will be able to see where the air bubbles come up, and we will be able to repair the hole and pump more air back in. The air that is still in the inner tube will keep forcing the inner tube up to the surface, and it might be too much for one or two people to hold down. I need help from everyone!"

With help from the rest of the class, she held Mr. Allen's inner tube under water and saw where the air was leaking. He repaired and refilled it and soon they were back on their way.

57

Water on the Mind

"I'm melting, I'm melting!" Svetlana complained.

"I feel like we are biking through the desert," Olga added as she lagged behind her sister, brother and father.

"I can't believe Mom kicked us out of the house for three hours so that she could have her book club meeting," Dmitri grumbled.

With nothing to do that afternoon, they had decided to go for a long bike ride. They had started on the trail of the old railroad line through the outskirts of town, which had been turned into a bike path, and then connected with some other paved trails. It had rained heavily for several days, but this summer day was sunny and hot and they were getting tired from the pedaling.

"Boy, you kids aren't exactly ready for the Tour de France," their father chuckled. "We'll be back to the car soon."

When they came to the bottom of a hill, Olga stopped to catch her breath and look around. "Look, look! There's a pond up ahead!" she said.

"Great! Let's all jump in!" Dmitri said.

"But we don't have bathing suits," Olga said.

"I don't care, I'm so hot I'll jump in with my clothes on," he said.

"I don't understand, how could there be a pond there?" Olga asked. "I've been here many times and there's never been a pond there."

"I hate to disappoint you guys," Svetlana said. "But it only looks like water. It's a mirage. The heat rising up from the paved path causes the shimmer that you see. The sunlight is being bent by hot air just above the ground so that it appears to be water. Keep pedaling, we'll be home soon."

Fill 'er Up

Gabriela and Mario's family had been saving for a trip to Italy for a long time. Their mother had relatives in Italy who they had never met, so they decided to combine visiting their relatives with sightseeing.

They started in Rome, where they saw the Colosseum and other ancient buildings. Next they took a bus trip to Pompeii. Then they rented a car for the rest of the vacation when they would be driving through the country. The car was smaller than the one they had at home and it was a tight fit with all four of them and their luggage, but everyone was enjoying the adventure.

On the second day of driving they needed gas for the car. Prices at all the gas stations they passed were similar, so they stopped at the next one. It advertised the price as a euro and thirty cents per liter.

"Okay, a euro is worth about a dollar and a quarter." Mario said as they pulled up to a pump. "So, a euro and thirty cents is less than two bucks. That's cheap."

"What do you mean?" Gabriela asked.

"Well, back home, gas is around four dollars a gallon. I'm surprised at the cost here," he said.

"It is a surprise, but not the kind you're thinking of," Gabriela said.

"At home, we measure gasoline in gallons, which is a standard measurement for volume. Here in Europe, they use the metric, rather than the standard system of weights and measures," Gabriela said. "A liter is only about a quarter of a gallon, roughly the size of a quart. So, instead of being cheaper than at home, gasoline here actually is much more expensive."

Rocks and Roles

"I can't believe I have to work on a school project over spring break," Amir grumbled.

"Well, if you had finished before we left home, you wouldn't have to be doing it now," his younger brother Hakim said.

Amir knew Hakim was right. The teacher had given the class several weeks to make a collection of something found in nature, and then to classify what they found. It was due the week after spring break.

Some kids had chosen to collect insects, others were collecting plants and some, like Amir, were collecting rocks.

"At least we came to a good place to finish your rock collection," Hakim said as the two of them walked along the beach. "This beach is full of different kinds of rocks."

"Stop talking and start collecting," Amir said. "I need five more kinds."

"Here's something that looks like quartz. And I'll bet this one is slate," Hakim said, picking up some stones.

"Good. Let's see, here's a piece of coral, here's something that I think is granite and this looks like sandstone," Amir said. "We're done."

"Are you sure you have enough?" Hakim asked.

"Yes, I only needed five more," Amir said. "Weren't you counting?"

"I was counting, that's why I know you don't have enough," Hakim said. "You need one more rock."

"What do you mean?" asked Amir.

"Quartz, slate, granite and sandstone are types of rock, but coral isn't," Hakim explained. "Coral is the skeleton produced by an ocean animal called a polyp. Coral reefs build up over the years from many generations of them stacking on top of each other. You still need to find one more kind of rock."

Weight Off Your Back

The students on the school newspaper staff met in the computer lab before school each Wednesday. The most recent issue had just been published and Oscar and Drake, who worked together on the editorial column, were trying to come up with a story for the next issue.

"My dad showed me an article last night saying kids should not carry backpacks that weigh more than fifteen percent of their weight," Drake said. "Otherwise, they can have all kinds of problems like back pain."

"We could do a story on that," Oscar said. "We could conduct a whole experiment where we bring in a bathroom scale, weigh kids and their backpacks and figure out how many are above that percentage."

Drake said, "And then we could interview the kids with the backpacks that weigh over fifteen percent of their body weight and ask if their backs ever hurt."

"I'm sure that heavy backpacks are a big problem in this school with as much homework as we get," Oscar said, sitting at the computer and starting to type. "I'll save time by getting the story started now. I already know what the conclusion of the article will be."

He began to type, "Many students in our school are suffering from back pain and other problems because their backpacks are too heavy."

"What do you think?" Oscar asked Drake, who was reading over his shoulder.

"I think it's too early to reach any conclusion, especially if we are trying to make this experiment follow the scientific method," Drake said.

"What do you mean?"

"We have a hypothesis: that some kids carry backpacks that weigh more than fifteen percent of their own weight," Drake explained. "We also have a neutral way to test that hypothesis, a way that others could repeat. But we need to conduct our experiment, collect data and analyze that data before we can conclude that some students have backpacks that weigh over fifteen percent of their body weight, let alone that overweight backpacks are causing back problems. Journalists, like scientists, need to be unbiased, and test their hypothesis before they come to a conclusion."

BONUS SECTION
Five More Minutes
of Science Mysteries!

Merry Experience

It was the Saturday after school ended, and Jasmine and Amari were looking forward to the city summer youth program, which was starting Monday at the community center.

They went to check out what was happening there. At the playground outside for younger kids, they saw a group of teenagers with paint and brushes.

"Is this your summer job?" Amari asked a teenager painting the monkey bars, each with a different color.

"We're getting the playground ready for the summer. It's actually an arts contest with an award for creativity," he said.

Another teenager was painting the legs of the swing sets with white and red stripes, making them look like big candy canes.

Jasmine and Amari walked to the merry-go-round. It was a large, round platform with handlebars on the outside to push and start it spinning, then to hold onto for the ride.

An older girl they knew named Sofia had painted the entire platform a pretty blue, but she looked dissatisfied.

"What's wrong?" Jasmine said.

"It's too plain. I'll never win with this," Sofia said.

"We can help," Amari said.

"Thanks, but I have to do all the painting for the contest myself," Sofia said.

"We won't do any of the painting," Jasmine said.

"Then how can you help?"

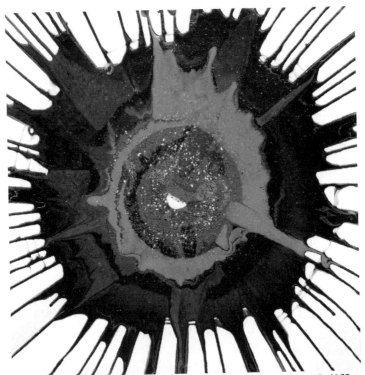

Amari replied, "We'll get a little of a couple of different color paints. We'll spin the merry-go-round as fast as we can get it going, and you reach over and dribble some paint on it, one color at a time."

"What will that do?" Sofia asked.

Jasmine said, "An object that is spinning behaves as if an outward force is being applied. The paint will spread toward the edge and it should make a wild pattern."

They did it and everyone loved the results, especially Sofia, who went on to win the award.

Clearing the Air

Even though they were cousins, Casper and Roger didn't see each other often because their families lived far apart. It had been a year since their last visit, when Roger's family had come from their home in Maine to see Casper's family in Florida during spring break.

On the first day of the visit, they had gone to a flower garden that Roger's mother wanted to see. There, Roger started sneezing and he didn't stop until they left.

They stayed in touch by text and online at times, but Casper still didn't know where Roger was going for spring break this year. The last he'd heard, several weeks before the break, Roger's family was thinking about either seeing other relatives in Georgia or else going skiing in Vermont.

When their mothers were finished talking on the phone one day soon after spring break, Casper got on the phone with Roger. "Did you go on a trip this year?" Casper asked.

"Sure did. And no sneezing this time," Roger said.

"How was the skiing?" Casper asked.

"How did you know we went skiing?" Roger asked.

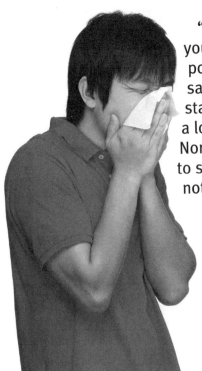

"Last year when you were here, you had an allergic reaction to the pollen from the flowers," Casper said. "Plants bloom in Southern states like Florida and Georgia a lot earlier than they do in the North. Anywhere it's cold enough to still be skiing, the plants would not be in bloom."

Oldies and Goodies

Benjamin, Kayla, Hailey and Logan enjoyed exploring their grandparents' big attic. There were trunks full of pictures and scrapbooks, dressers with clothes, cassette players, televisions with picture tubes, telephones with dials and much more.

The school yard sale was coming up and their grandparents had said each of them could pick something to donate.

Hailey chose a brass lamp that had a fancy, frilly shade, although the electrical wire was frayed. Benjamin found a program from a World Series game long ago. Kayla decided on a woman's hat painted with a beach scene. Logan picked out an old mirror with a thermometer attached to it. The silver liquid in the thermometer read 96 degrees.

"Let's go. It's too hot to stay up here," Logan said.

They climbed down the stairs and showed the things to their grandparents.

"Actually," said their grandmother, looking over their spoils, "you've picked one thing that we wouldn't want you to sell."

"Probably it's this lamp with the bare wire," Hailey said. "You might get an electric shock if you plugged it in."

"I think she means this baseball game program is too rare to give up," Benjamin said.

"This hat looks like it's hand-painted, so that could be valuable," Kayla said. "Or is the mirror a collectible?"

"The thermometer on the mirror probably has mercury in it. Mercury is one of the few metals that is liquid at room temperature," Logan said. "It expands and contracts depending on the temperature. Years ago, it was used in thermometers like colored alcohol is used today."

"I forgot we still had that," their grandmother said. "People didn't know it at the time, but mercury is very dangerous, even to breathe its fumes. If that thermometer broke, the mercury would spill out. We don't want anyone taking that risk. We'll take it to the hazardous waste disposal center."

"I'll replace the wire on that lamp and then you can donate it with the other things," their grandfather added. "I have lots of old baseball programs, and your grandma has never worn that hat in all the years since I bought it for her. Meanwhile, let's find something else for you to donate, Logan."

Keep a Balanced Diet

The student council had a new idea for organizing the school's annual collection for the local food bank: they decided to make an actual "food pyramid" with the donations. Even though the new posters used a plate to show a balanced diet, the old-style food pyramid worked better for displaying the donations.

The students had moved an extra set of shelves from the library into the entrance lobby. As kids brought in items, they put them in the correct places. There were carbohydrates like crackers and pasta on the bottom shelf, the next shelf held various dried fruits on one side and canned vegetables on the other. On the third shelf were dairy products like powdered milk and parmesan cheese on the left and a place for protein on the right. The fourth and highest shelf was for sweets and fatty things.

That day, it was Fleur's turn to help the younger kids put their donations in the right place as they came to school. Three kindergarteners came in together carrying baked beans, sunflower seeds, and canned tuna.

"Go ahead and put all of those things next to the beef jerky," Fleur said. "Do you need any help reaching it?"

The kindergarteners looked at each other in confusion.

"Why do all of these things go on the same shelf?" one of them asked.

"And next to the beef jerky? They're not meat," said the second.

"Yeah, the beans and seeds are plants. Shouldn't they go with the fruits or vegetables or something?" added the third.

Fleur chuckled. "Yes, they are all different, but they are all proteins. Beans and seeds are plants but they contain a lot of protein just like poultry, red meat, and fish. Animal products are a great way to get protein, but they aren't the only way."

Tanks a Lot

When Giselle and Camilla finally got the aquarium they had wanted in their room, their mother reminded them that they had promised to take good care of the fish.

"You need to replace a third of the water every week," she said as they set up the tank. "And once a month, put the fish in another container, clean everything and put in all new water."

"That sounds like two equal jobs," Giselle said when the girls were alone later. "One person changes a third of the water every week and the other does the complete change once a month. Doesn't matter to me. Take your pick."

"I'll change a third of the water every week," Camilla said.

"Deal," Giselle said.

"And I'll do it the easy way," Camilla added.

"What do you mean?" Giselle asked.

"I won't have to take out old water," Camilla said. "I'll just leave the top off the tank. Over a week, about that much will evaporate. Then all I'll need to do is put in the fresh water."

"That's not fair!" Giselle said.

"Sorry, we had a deal," Camilla said.

"I mean it's not fair to the fish," Giselle said.

"What do you mean, not fair to the fish?" Camilla asked.

"The point of changing water is that you're taking out some of the old water that has gotten dirty from uneaten food and from the fish living in the water," Giselle said. "If you just let water evaporate, the dirty stuff stays in the water left behind and it's even worse for the fish because it's more concentrated."

"Okay, I'll take out old water," Camilla said. "We've been asking for these fish for a long time and we should take care of them the right way."

Discover
One Minute Mysteries:
65 Short Mysteries
You Solve With Math!

All Wound Up

"No way, a real wind-up watch? One that ticks and everything?" Ian asked.

"I think I saw one of those in an old movie once," Wyatt said.

Hector was showing off a watch that had been in his family for many years and was a family treasure.

"My grandfather gave it to me today," Hector said. "It was right at noon. He showed me how to set the hands and wound it one turn of this little wheel on the side to start it."

"Are you sure it works, though?" Wyatt asked. For the first time, Hector noticed that the watch was not running. Its hands showed three o'clock, and it was now four o'clock.

"Well, I guess I have to wind it again," Hector said.

"Isn't that going to be a lot of trouble?" Ian asked. "I mean, winding it again and again every day."

"I don't think it will be that often," Hector said. He started winding the watch, counting sixteen turns until it was fully wound. "In fact, I can tell you exactly when it will need to be wound again."

"When is that?" Wyatt asked.

"Four o'clock, the day after tomorrow," Hector answered.

"How do you figure that?" Ian asked.

"Well, my grandfather started it by winding it one turn, and it ran for three hours," Hector said. "I just now wound it all the way, sixteen turns, which means that when you wind it fully it will run for 48 hours before stopping—sixteen times three. Winding it every other day isn't too much trouble, especially since it means so much to me."

# Chute in the Works

On Saturday morning, Caleb rode up the bike path to his friend Patrick's house. That morning Patrick was in his yard painting a model rocket. As much as Caleb loved bicycle riding—he had a bike with a speedometer, lights, water bottle holder and other accessories—Patrick loved model rockets.

"Cool," Caleb said, admiring his friend's new rocket.

"Maybe too cool to use," Patrick said.

Patrick and his father belonged to a club that launched model rockets. Sometimes, though, rockets crashed and broke apart because their parachutes didn't open. The parachute for Patrick's new rocket was already attached to the nose cone.

"I'm worried about this parachute," Patrick said. "The instructions say it should open when the rocket hits 30 miles an hour on the descent. I've tried to test it, but I guess I can't throw the nose cone that fast."

"I'll take it on a ride down the bike path," Caleb suggested. "Once I get going that fast, we'll know if it will open or not."

Caleb tried several times but could never get the parachute to open.

"Sorry, I can't get this bicycle going more than about 20 miles an hour," Caleb said when he returned.

"I have an idea," Patrick said. "And I wouldn't suggest this if you weren't a good enough biker to handle it."

"What do you have in mind?" Caleb asked.

"Once you get going on your bike, throw the nose cone forward," Patrick said. "The speed of the throw will be added to the speed of the bicycle. So if you're riding at 20 miles an hour and you throw it at even just 10 miles an hour, it will be moving forward at 30 miles an hour, and you'll see if it opens."

Caleb did just that. It was a little tricky since he had to steer with only one hand and throw with the other, but it worked. The parachute opened.

"Now it's time for lift-off!" Patrick said.

Ace of Clubs

3

Natalie and her father had been taking golf lessons. They were hitting the ball pretty well, so they thought it was time to go out and play their first real round of golf.

On the first hole, they hit their drives down the fairway.

"This marker says we're 150 yards out from the green, Daddy," Natalie said when they reached his ball.

"Okay, the instructor said 150 yards is how far I hit with a six-iron," her father said, pulling out that club. He took a practice swing that was interrupted when his hat flew off back toward the tee, making Natalie laugh.

He hit the shot the way he usually did, but it landed 30 yards short of the green. "I could have sworn he told me I hit six-irons 150 yards," he said.

The next hole ran parallel to that one, but going the other way. After their drives, Natalie's father was once again about 150 yards from the green. "Let's see, the instructor said there's about a 15-yard difference in how far different clubs send the ball, and the lower the number of the club the farther the ball goes. So if I hit the six-iron 120 yards like I did on the last hole, I'll need to use the longer club that will hit it 30 more yards. That means a four-iron," he said.

"On the first hole you hit a shot that normally would travel about 150 yards," she said. "That shot was into the wind. You hit a good shot, but it still only went 120 yards. So, the wind reduced the distance of your shot by 30 yards, or a fifth.

"On this hole, we're going the opposite direction, meaning the wind is behind us. So the wind will add about one-fifth to the distance of your shot. So hit the club tahat normally makes the ball go about 120 yards, and let the wind push it. Since you usually hit the six-iron 150 yards, and each higher numbered club sends the ball 15 yards less, you should use an eight-iron."

Cold Blooded Calculations

4

Henry was so excited that his parents had finally allowed him to get a pet iguana. They went to the pet store that day, and when they got there he ran straight to the tanks.

Henry had already picked out a medium-sized iguana, and he had things for the iguana to climb on. So he just needed a tank. "Okay, easy enough," he thought.

He wanted to give it as much room to climb around as he could. There were three sizes of tanks. One had a base of 16 by 24 inches and was 12 inches high. The other had a base 16 by 16 inches and was 20 inches high. Another had a base of 20 by 20 inches and was 12 inches high. The cost of each tank was about the same.

Henry looked at the tanks for only a moment. "I'll take this one. It has the most space," he said, pointing to one of them.

"How did you figure that out so fast?" his father asked.

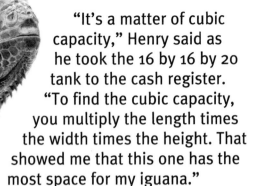

"It's a matter of cubic capacity," Henry said as he took the 16 by 16 by 20 tank to the cash register. "To find the cubic capacity, you multiply the length times the width times the height. That showed me that this one has the most space for my iguana."

"Yes, but how could you do it in your head so fast?" his father asked. "I think I'd need a pencil and paper for that."

"To get the exact number, yes," Henry said. "But we only needed to compare, so I simplified the calculations. Each of the dimensions was divisible by four. With the 16 by 24 by 12 tank, if you divide each number by 4 you're left with 4 by 6 by 3—72. The 20 by 20 by 12 tank becomes 5 by 5 by 3—75. The 16 by 16 by 20 tank becomes 4 by 4 by 5—80. That's the biggest of the three."

As they drove home, Henry got out a pencil and paper to check the exact figures. "The 20 by 20 by 12 tank is 4,800 cubic inches," he said. "The 16 by 24 by 12 tank is 4,608 cubic inches. The 16 by 16 by 20 tank is 5,120 cubic inches. That is the biggest, and it should give my new iguana plenty of room."

And They Call This a Fair?

Mrs. Grabowski's class was working at the school fair to help raise money for new supplies for the math room. Kendall and her best friend Ruby decided to make a game with 20 rectangles of flat cardboard that were three inches long and two inches wide.

The sign on their table said:

Win a prize by proving you know which way these rectangles can be arranged to cover the most area.

Two boys they knew, Micah and Sean, tried five times. Mrs. Grabowski, the judge, rejected all the different arrangements they made.

"This game is impossible," Micah said.

"Maybe to you, Micah, but it really is possible," Ruby said.

After the fair was over and nobody had won, Sean came up to Ruby and Kendall.

"Okay, what's the correct answer?" he asked.

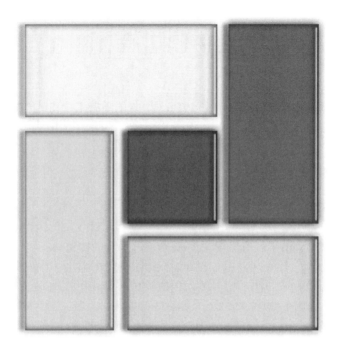

"Remember, the goal was to prove you know which way they cover the most area," Kendall said. "They cover the same area no matter how you arrange them. All you had to do was say that."

Index

A

absorb, 100
air
    pollution, 128
    pressure, 82, 86
temperature, 102, 122
allergic reaction, 148
arachnid, 120
area, 165, 166
atmosphere, 63, 108

B

baking
    powder, 82
    soda, 82
bike, 159
biology, 39

C

camouflage, 30
carbohydrate, 151
cell
    membrane, 28
    wall, 28
chloroplast, 28
chlorophyll, 28
clouds
    nimbostratus, 66
    cirrus, 66
    cumulonimbus, 66
cold, 66
club, 161
concentrated, 154
condense, 58
contract, 150
cookies, 81, 82
Coral Reef, 59
cubic capacity, 164
cytoplasm, 28

D

diameter, 72
diamond, 91, 92
density, 116
dissolve, 95

E

earth
    axis, 52
    core, 54
    rotation, 60
eclipse, 55, 56
ecosystem, 57
elasticity, 86
electricity, 60, 127
elevation, 82, 108
energy
    kinetic, 106
    potential, 106
    solar, 128
environment, 50, 60
erosion, 61
eruption, 53
evaporate, 82, 118, 154
evaporation, 122, 153
exoskeleton, 44
expand, 150

F

filters, 114
fire, 108
frequency, sound, 110

G

gas, 82
gasoline, 137, 138
geothermic activity, 54
geyser, 53
granite, 140
gravitational pull, 68
gravity, 70, 75

H

high elevation, 82
helium, 97
hot springs, 53, 54
hour, 157
humidity, 118
hypothesis, 142

I

iguana, 163, 164
inches, 163, 164
insect, 120, 139
invertebrate, 44

K

kinetic energy, 106

L

leavening agents, 82
life cycle, 26
life expectancy, 40
light, visible, 100
lighter, 107, 108
lunar eclipse, 55

M

magnetic, 123, 124
mammal, 20, 119, 120
metal, 124, 150

metamorphosis, 26, 42
meteorite, 64
metric system, 138
migrate, 32
migration, 19
mildew, 130
mineral hardness, 92
mirage, 136
moisture, 118, 122
molecule, 94

O

Old Faithful, 53
orbit, 68, 64
outward force, 146
oxygen, 20, 103, 108

P

parachutes, 159
phototropism, 36
planet, 49, 71, 75, 76
polar, 50
pollen, 148
pollinate, 18
polyp, 140
precipitate, 96
predator, 29
protein, 151

Q

quartz, 140

R

radiate, 74, 100
rainbow, 83, 84
rainforest, 77
reaction, 104
rectangle, 165
reflect, 100, 126
rocket, model, 159

S

T

V

W

Y

Z

Photo and Illustration Credits

About the Authors

Eric Yoder is a writer and editor who has been published in a variety of magazines, newspapers, newsletters and online publications on science, government, law, business, sports and other topics. He has written, contributed to or edited numerous books, mainly in the areas of employee benefits and financial planning. A reporter at the *Washington Post*, he is also the award-winning coauthor, along with his daughter, Natalie, of the first two books in the wildly popular series: *65 Short Mysteries You Solve With Science!* and *65 Short Mysteries You Solve With Math!* He and his wife, Patti, enjoy spending time with their two daughters, Natalie and Valerie. He can be reached at Eric@ScienceNaturally.com.

Natalie Yoder, who wrote these stories while a high school student, is now a college student studying communications. She has been featured in news stories, on National Public Radio and on web sites for mystery writers and fans, following publication of *One Minute Mysteries: 65 Short Mysteries You Solve with Science!* and *One Minute Mysteries: 65 Short Mysteries You Solve with Math!* She continues to write in her free time and is excited about the publication of her third book. She can be reached at Natalie@ScienceNaturally.com.

Check out our other great books:

One Minute Mysteries:
65 Short Mysteries You Solve With Math!

By Eric Yoder and Natalie Yoder

The second book in our wildly successful "One Minute Mysteries" series, *One Minute Mysteries: 65 Short Mysteries You Solve With Math!* keeps you entertained and eager to learn more. These short mysteries, each just one minute long, have a fun and interesting twist—you have to tap into your mathematical wisdom to solve them! These brain twisters challenge your knowledge of math in everyday life!

As much fun as the first book in the series, *One Minute Mysteries: 65 Short Mysteries You Solve With Science!*, this educational book is easy to use at home, in school or even in the car. Great for kids, grown-ups, educators and anyone who loves good mysteries, good math problems or both!

"...real-life situations with solutions that would make Encyclopedia Brown jealous." —Clay Kaufman, Co-Director, Siena School

"...fabulous resource for kids, parents and teachers looking for a way to link mathematics to everyday life."
—Carole Basile, Ed.D., University of Colorado, Denver

Ages 10-14
ISBN 10: 0-967802-00-8
Paperback $9.95
E-book ISBN 10: 0-9700106-5-6
Braille: visit www.BrailleIntl.org
Coming soon in Chinese and Korean!

101 *Things Everyone Should Know About Science*

By Dia L. Michels and Nathan Levy

Best Books Award FINALIST!
USA Book News

"**Succinct, cleverly written...should be on everyone's bookshelf!**"
—Katrina L. Kelner, Ph.D. *Science* Magazine

"**Readers will devour the book and be left eager for the 102ⁿᵈ thing to know!**" —Margaret Kenda, *Science Wizardry for Kids*

Why do you see lightning before you hear thunder? What keeps the planets orbiting around the Sun? Why do we put salt on roads when they are icy? What metal is a liquid at room temperature? And the burning question: Why do so many scientists wear white lab coats?

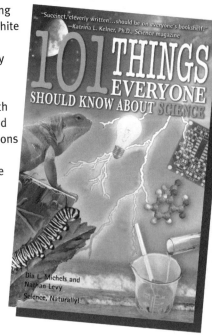

Science affects everything—yet so many of us wish we understood it better. Using an engaging question-and-answer format, key concepts in biology, chemistry, physics, earth science and general science are explored and demystified. Endorsed by science organizations and educators, this easy-to-tackle book is a powerful tool to assess and increase science literacy. Perfect for kids, parents, educators and anyone interested in gaining a better understanding of how science impacts everyday life.

Ages 8-12
ISBN 10: 0-967802-05-9
Paperback $9.95
E-book ISBN 10: 0-9700106-6-4
Braille: visit www.BrailleIntl.org
Coming Soon in Chinese and Korean!

101 *Things Everyone Should Know About Math*
By Marc Zev, Kevin Segal, and Nathan Levy

Endorsed by the National Council of Teachers of Mathematics

"A wonderful book for making complex topics approachable and helping readers discover the fascinating world of math!"
—Rachel Connelly, Ph.D. Economics, Bowdoin College

Fun, FREE educational App Helps Kids Enjoy Math!

101 Math is a new iPhone/ iPad/ iPod app that uses the appeal of electronics to keep kids excited about the next math problem!

Available in the iTunes App Store!

Math is a critical part of our everyday lives. The second title in the award-winning "101 Things Everyone Should Know" series helps you understand how you use math dozens of times—every day. With entertaining connections to sports, hobbies, science, food, and travel, mathematical concepts are simplified and explained using clear, real-life explanations. You'll even learn some fun trivia and math history! Using an engaging question and answer format, this book is perfect for kids, parents, educators, and anyone interested in the difference between an Olympic event score of 9.0 and Richter scale score of 9.0.

Ages 10-14
ISBN 10: 0-967802-03-2
Paperback $9.95
E-book ISBN 10: 0-9700106-3-X
Coming Soon in Chinese and Korean!

If My Mom Were a Platypus:
Mammal Babies and Their Mothers

By Dia L. Michels • Illustrated by Andrew Barthelmes

"As engaging visually as it is verbally!"
—Dr. Ines Cifuentes, Carnegie Academy for Science Education

"The animal facts . . . are completely engrossing. Most readers are sure to be surprised by something they learn about these seemingly familiar animals."
—Carolyn Baile, *ForeWord* magazine

Learn how 14 mammals are born, eat, sleep, learn and mature. The fascinating facts depict how mammal infants begin life dependent on their mothers and grow to be self-sufficient adults. This book highlights the topics of birth, growth, knowledge and eating for 13 different animals. All stories are told from the baby's point of view. The 14th and final species is a human infant, with amazing similarities to the other stories. With stunning full color and black-and-white illustrations and concise information, this book helps children develop a keen sense of what makes mammals special.

Ages 8-12, 64 pages. Curriculum-based Activity Guide with dozens of fun, hands-on projects available free of charge at www.ScienceNaturally.com

English paperback	ISBN 10: 1-930775-19-9	$9.95
Spanish paperback	ISBN 10: 0-9700106-8-0	$9.95
Dutch paperback	ISBN 10: 1-930775-46-6	$16.95
Hebrew hardback	ISBN 10: 0-9678020-8-3	$16.95

Add a 12" Plush Platypus Toy to any order for just $11.00!
Visit www.ScienceNaturally.com for details.

About Science, Naturally!

Science, Naturally! is an independent press located in Washington, DC. We are committed to increasing science and math literacy by exploring and demystifying topics in entertaining and enlightening ways. Our products are filled with interesting facts, important insights and key connections in math and science. We try to make potentially intimidating topics intriguing and accessible to scientists and mathematicians of all ages. Our books, booklets and apps are perfect for kids, parents, educators and anyone interested in gaining a better understanding of how science and math affect everyday life.

Our materials are designed to engage readers by using both fiction and nonfiction strategies to teach potentially intimidating subjects. Our book content correlates to the national science and math standards set out by the Center for Education at the National Academies (articulations available on our website). All our books have received the coveted "Recommends" designation from the National Science Teachers Association and our math books have been endorsed by the National Council of Teachers of Mathematics. Our award-winning books have been designated as superb supplemental resources for home education and science teachers alike.

Science, Naturally! books are distributed by National Book Network in the U.S. and abroad, and by Mariposa Press in France. Many of our titles are available in Spanish, Dutch, Chinese and Korean.

For more information about our publications, to request a catalog, to be added to our mailing list or to learn more about becoming a *Science, Naturally!* author, give us a call or visit us online.

Bridging the gap between
the blackboard and the blacktop

Science, Naturally!®
725 8th Street, SE
Washington, DC 20003
202-465-4798
Toll-free: 1-866-SCI-9876
(1-866-724-9876)
Fax: 202-558-2132
Info@ScienceNaturally.com
www.ScienceNaturally.com
www.Facebook.com/ScienceNaturally
www.Twitter.com/SciNaturally